Song of the Meadowlark

Song of the
Meadowlark

**Exploring Values for a
Sustainable Future**

JAMES EGGERT

Illustrations by Sally Rogers

TEN SPEED PRESS
Berkeley, California

TEN SPEED PRESS
P.O. Box 7123
Berkeley, California 94707
www.tenspeed.com

Distributed in Australia by Simon and Schuster Australia, in Canada by Ten Speed Press Canada, in New Zealand by Tandem Press, in South Africa by Real Books, in Southeast Asia by Berkeley Books, and in the United Kingdom and Europe by Airlift Books.

Cover design by Gary Bernal
Cover illustration (meadowlark) by Sandra Starck
Cover photo © The Image Bank
Interior design by Jeff Brandenburg, ImageComp
Illustrations by Sally Rogers

Grateful acknowledgment to the following publications and publishers which had originally published earlier versions of this book's essays: *The Washington Post*, *Challenge*, *Jump River Review*, *North Country Anvil*, *Craft Report*, *Elementary Teachers' Ideas and Materials Workshop*, *Heartland Journal*, Burning Gate Press, & M. E. Sharpe.

Library of Congress Cataloging-in-Publication Data on file with the publisher.

First printing, 1999
Printed in Canada

1 2 3 4 5 6 7 8 9 10 — 03 02 01 00 99

With love to Anthony and Leslie, and to my father, Bob Eggert, who has a passion for learning.

Contents

Foreword

This is an unusual and valuable book in many respects. Its author, of course, is an economist, but not one devoted to the prevailing theology of his profession. Economists mostly work with the dedication of beavers or bees toward the great goal of More. *Growth, expansion, acceleration* are the sacred words of their creed. And the economists have been enormously successful; their faith has spread around the world, crowding out all other creeds.

Yet there is always something rather, well, dismal about the field of economics. This comes, I think, from its disciples' firm determination to wall off certain questions. For instance, "What makes for happiness?" or "How do I figure out what I want from life?" They can answer these only by pointing to our consumer behavior: We must want what we buy. But they must sense the tautological absurdity of that line of argument.

Now comes James Eggert, one of a small school of economists that has begun to think outside the box. And it is curious that he begins by examining a word long used by his tribe: *value*. He imbues it—marvelously—with real meaning, instead of the stale and transactional definition to be found in the front of the econ textbooks. "Their song is pleasing, their color and swoop of flight enchanting." Suddenly we are using good old nouns and adjectives, sweet and solid Anglo-Saxon words instead of the ponderous

Latinate syllables of the professional journals. These things are *valuable* he insists. And if you assign them a value in your heart, then you are in a position to begin to assess other developments—the "efficiency," for instance, of the modern farm, which leaves no room for the meadowlarks to nest and fledge their young.

This book rambles inefficiently along, which is why it is a good and true book, full of things to talk about with your friends and family, and with yourself. The essays are lighthearted and smart, never didactic and never crystal-gazing or New Agey; the author, after all, is from Wisconsin. Instead there are delightful discussions of repair, of high jumping, of topsoil, of many things that constitute a joyful and complete human life.

Song of the Meadowlark will be of great use to all who read it, but it would be especially helpful—though subversive—to give it to anyone you know to have been born an economist. It will help them see that they've been focused on one small patch of the whole and that there really is more to life.

—BILL MCKIBBEN

Preface

. . . the basic nature of the universe . . . may be described as a universal field, whose most essential quality is unbroken wholeness in flowing movement . . . this suggests that the whole is a primary notion, while the parts are abstractions from the whole. . . .

—DAVID BOHM

If you're lucky, you can still hear the song of the meadowlark, although in some places their music is becoming less common. And if you are still, and listen carefully, you may hear more than the meadowlark's flutelike, enchanting melody. You might also hear something about ourselves as well—something about our technologies and economics, about Earth's natural balances and imbalances, about wholeness and joy, and of our long-ago evolutionary histories and shared futures.

Song of the Meadowlark is one economist's ruminations, thought journeys, and (I confess) sometimes quirky essays—all dedicated to exploring themes loosely related to holistic values, values often made invisible to our conventional business and economics world. Metaphorically (in honor of our "mentor bird"), I will refer to this theme as a quest for "meadowlark values."

Among other things, meadowlark values include a commitment to preserving the diversity of all life forms and, if possible, maintaining the health of human, cultural, and natural ecosystems. The first chapter addresses specific environmental problems that are not easily resolved within our current economic environment. I also suggest how we might create a broader perspective than strict, conventional market economics. What would it mean, for example, if one were committed to becoming a "meadowlark economist"—someone who understands the principles of economics and can also combine that understanding with an intimate awareness and respect for ecological principles?

In addition, meadowlark values lead us to rethink other economic, social, and individual issues—our practices of education, our habits of consumption, our attitudes toward work, or simply the way we live.

At a deeper level, a commitment to meadowlark values insists that we go one step further, to explore our joint "epic of evolution"[1] including a new perspective of who we are and what humans share with Earth's other creatures within our common history of cosmological and biological evolution. The final essays will thus serve as a primer on our evolutionary background as we explore the age-old question of our place in the universe. The chapters "A Cosmic Journey," "Of Time and Place," and "The Copycat Species" provide an orientation and a context for the concluding essay: a meditation on human purpose and possibility.

I wish to dedicate this book, most simply, to the meadowlarks who sing by day and to the little frogs who sing so beautifully in the night. I would also like to dedicate the book to the children who delight in such songs, and finally to our grandchildren, who may continue to enjoy their natural affinities and who will continue to listen and learn from the song of the meadowlark.

Acknowledgments

A heartfelt thank-you to all those who helped with this book's manuscript and production—especially those who provided (at propitious moments) critical doses of encouragement, helpful ideas, or some new perspective as the book took form through various stages of evolution.

More specifically, I wish to thank Larry Lynch who, early on, helped give the manuscript a sense of purpose and direction. Also thanks to Sally Rogers, Sandra Starck, Jeff Davis, Parker Huber, Karl Avery, Cynthia Casey, Ken Salway, Brian Bansenauer, Leonard Lahaye, Richard Eggert, Paul Edmondson, John Medelman, Jeff Davis, Eugene Soroko, Tom Richards, Jean Hoff, Paul Thomas, Mark Mosey, Van Foreman, Paul Roques, Richard Damro, Dave Bauer, Scott Housenga, Peder Hamm, Ken Parejko, Joe Johnson, Bea Bigony, my wife Pat, my daughter Leslie, and my father Bob Eggert.

Last but not least, I would like to thank publisher Phil Wood, project editor Jason Rath, and the rest of the production staff at Ten Speed Press for taking on this project and, with enthusiasm and artistry, orchestrating the disparate elements of this book into its completed form—a warm thanks to you all.

PART ONE

MEADOWLARK VALUES
Economics, Education, and Ecology

A thing is right when it tends to preserve the integrity, stability, and beauty of the biotic community. It is wrong when it tends otherwise.

—ALDO LEOPOLD

CHAPTER 1

Meadowlark Economics

By the power of our imagination we can sense the future generations breathing with the rhythm of our own breath or feel them hovering like a cloud of witnesses. Sometimes I fancy that if I were to turn my head suddenly, I would glimpse them over my shoulder.

—JOANNA MACY

Considering the problems we face at the dawn of the twenty-first century—and the evolution of values we're seeing in response—I sometimes wonder about the competency of contemporary economists. This may seem like an odd comment from someone who has spent the past twenty-eight years teaching economics. Indeed, I've defended my discipline's importance to my students and others on countless occasions.

What exactly is the economist's special contribution? Our stock-in-trade includes the following: recognizing scarcity and the importance of incentives, helping to make choices, identifying trade-offs, and making connections (that may not always be obvious) between the larger economy and one's own small, individual, economic world.

On the last point, I recall a class in the mid-1980s when a student asked what I meant by "making connections." The same day, nature, fortuitously, had provided me with an interesting and unusual example. I told the students that I had trouble getting to school that morning because a couple of aspen trees near a dammed-up marshy area had been cut overnight and had blocked the roadway.

"Now what," I asked, "did international trade and finance have to do with these downed trees and my morning's frustration?" Working it through, we concluded that there may have been the following connections:

> ➤ Who cut the trees? Probably beavers.

> ➤ Why were they felling trees near the road? Overpopulation.

> ➤ Why were there too many beavers? No trapping that year.

> ➤ What happened to the beaver pelt market? Decreased sales in overseas markets.

> ➤ Why did the sales decrease? Because of the high value of the U.S. dollar in the spring of 1985.

Some of the fun of teaching is thinking through such illustrations, examining the connective tissue of the Big Economy and world markets, and then trying to see how they relate to little you and me. Indeed, most economists are trained to do this kind of analysis quite well.

So what is our shortcoming?

I believe it is simply this: We economists have simply not gone far enough in broadening our understanding of ecology and ecological values.

Ecology and Economics

The words economics and ecology have the same prefix: eco, from the Greek *oikos*, which literally means "household." The original definition of economics implied an understanding, a caring for, and the management of human households, whereas *ecology* implied an understanding and appreciation of the interrelationships within nature's "household." I believe these two households are becoming more interdependent and their futures more and more intimately linked. When we fail to calculate ecological values or see the connections, we pave the way for losses that are both unintended and unwanted. One example (on a small scale to be sure) is now occurring where I live, a dairy farming region of the upper Midwest. We are losing our meadowlarks!

Those of us who walk or jog or bike along our rural roads enjoy the few meadowlarks that are left. Their song is pleasing, their color and swoop of flight enchanting. The complete disappearance of meadowlarks would, plain and simple, be wrong, and would diminish the quality of our lives.

Why are we losing the meadowlarks? Most likely they are disappearing as a result of haylage—a modern method of haying. Farmers now tend to cut their hay "green" with minimal drying, early in the spring. They then put it into a wagon and blow it into the silo. Years ago, most farmers let their hay grow longer—perhaps two to three weeks longer—before cutting it. It was then dried and raked into windrows before baling. This method gave field-nesting birds (such as meadowlarks and bobolinks) time to establish a brood and fledge their young before the mower arrived on the scene.

Haylage, in turn, is an offshoot of improved farm "efficiency," of substituting machinery for labor and of minimizing time and costly rain delays that characterized the old cutting/drying/baling method.

These changes took place with the blessings of ag economists, university researchers, on down the line to the county extension agent. But in the meantime, who was valuing the meadowlarks?

Despite the intrinsic value of their sweet song, these birds have no voice economically or politically. They represent a zero within our conventional economic accounting system (we don't even buy birdseed or build birdhouses for meadowlarks). Their disappearance and the loss of such meadowlark values would not create even the tiniest ripple in the Commerce Department spreadsheets that are supposed to measure our standard of living.

Meadowlark Values

In truth, there are meadowlark values (as opposed to strict economic values) everywhere—in estuaries and sand dunes, in wetlands and woodlands, in native prairies and Panamanian rain forests. Quite probably the quality of your own life is, to some degree, dependent on these values. They are on every continent; they can be seen upstate and downstate. Just look around, and you will find them (like our meadowlarks) on your road, or next door, or perhaps in your own backyard.

Meadowlark values were underrepresented when some members of Congress tried to open up the Arctic National Wildlife Refuge for oil and gas exploration. Meadowlark values were shortchanged when economists pointed out (quite correctly) that Exxon's massive oil spill in Alaska actually *increased* our gross domestic product (by putting billions of dollars into the cleanup and thereby fattening paychecks as well as state and national income).

Perhaps it is time we economists begin to rethink our strict adherence to dollar and GDP values. We should not, of course, discard our old and valuable skills: recognizing scarcity and the power of economic incentives, making efficient choices, and pointing out trade-offs. But perhaps we need to broaden our thinking to create a new kind of economist, someone who can incorporate ecological thinking and ecological values with market thinking and market values—a true meadowlark economist if you will.

I'm ashamed to admit that I took my first elementary class in ecology after teaching economics for more than two decades. I still have a ways to go. I am now beginning to read (and appreciate) some of the latter-day economists who represent such new thinking: Ken Boulding, Hazel Henderson, Robert Heilbroner, Herman Daly, Lester Brown, Leopold Kohr, and E. F. Schumacher, to name a few.

In addition, I hope that more and more prominent economists—at the level of Milton Friedman, Robert Solow, Campbell R. McConnell, Louis Rukeyser, Dick Armey, and Alan Greenspan—of today and of the future, will feel comfortable not only with traditional market/growth economics, but will also know something of ecology as well, will value the integrity of the environment along with the "bottom line," will promote development as well as protect the standard of living of the other organisms with whom we share the planet.

Along with environmental impact statements (EIS), perhaps future economists can devise what might be called GIS or "grandchild impact statements," making sure our kids and their kids will have sustainable quantities of biological and other resources, helping preserve our soils and waters, fisheries and forests, whales and bluebirds—even the tiny toads and butterflies—and ensuring that these entities will have their voices represented.

Meadowlark Economics

So to all you National Association of Business Economists, government advisers, and teachers, too: Let's dedicate ourselves to a new standard of—what?—meadowlark economics, of protecting and sustaining for the future a larger and more comprehensive set of durable values.

CHAPTER 2

Topsoil Drama

The care of the earth is our most ancient and most worthy and, after all, our most pleasing responsibility. To cherish what remains of it, and to foster its renewal, is our only legitimate hope.

—WENDELL BERRY

Topsoil, we know, makes life possible on this planet. Yet how many of us know that creating topsoil is a slow, slow process and losing it can be dishearteningly swift? Surely these are important facts for all of us to know, and especially important to impress upon young people.

With this in mind, I felt that a natural history of soils might be a useful, and even fun, topic when my wife asked me to do a project for her Girl Scout day camp. Starting with a suggestion from Del Thomas, a local soil scientist, we decided to create a play. In addition, we tried to make the drama relatively simple, so others might try it (or some variation of it) with a minimum of cost and preparation. Here then is an account of what we did:

We gathered twenty girls, aged seven to twelve, for a one-hour activity. I began by suggesting they pick up some topsoil, and then asked,

"How important is this in keeping you alive?" This question created an excellent opportunity for all of us to think through the essential nature of what we negatively refer to as "dirt." Of course, all our vegetables, our fruit, and our grains are directly dependent upon soil, and most everything else we eat is indirectly dependent upon it as well.

How about a pizza? How do the ingredients, including the meat, directly or indirectly depend on topsoil? What about lumber for our homes, paper for books and writing, cotton and wool to keep us warm? What about butterflies and bumblebees, foxes and meadowlarks? Yes, all of us depend on a food chain that begins with the miracle of water, sunlight, and seeds combined with this dark, crumbly substance ever present under our feet.

Next question: "Where does soil come from?" Here I brought out a jar of water with a tablespoon of alum mixed in. (The alum, which can be purchased at a grocery store, helps separate the various soil components.) We then put a handful of our collected soil into the water, screwed the lid tight, and let everyone give the jar a shake. Within a minute it became obvious that our soil had at least three components: first, the small stones and sand that remained on the bottom; next, the silty or fine clay particles of the middle; and finally, the decomposed vegetable matter floating on top. After we observed this, I asked the girls if they would like to be in a play in which we would "make" some soil.

"Yes," they shouted unanimously.

"OK, let's begin at the beginning, with rock (probably from a volcano), which, over time, is broken up by Wind and Water. Which of you wants to be a volcano?" Many hands shot up. I chose a volunteer and placed a prepared "Volcano" sign around her neck. From my son's rock collection, I had brought along a sample of volcanic rock, a hand-sized piece of lightweight pumice. We passed it around and then gave it back to the girl designated "Volcano."

"Anyone want to be Water?" I got a couple of volunteers and gave them "Water" signs. "Now who wants to be Wind?"

I explained that wind and water "will act on these rocks, as they did over billions of years, to break up the volcanic rock into smaller and smaller pieces of sand and stone." I also pointed out that these

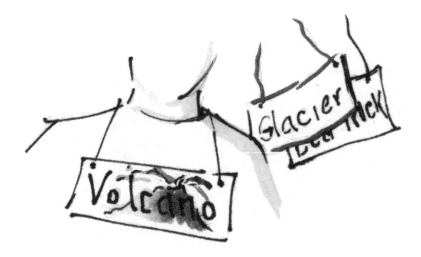

sand particles were carried about over long periods of time, mainly by water, and eventually came to rest. There they sat. With more and more sand coming in, compressing the bottom, the layers became tightly packed together, as if they were cemented or glued.

This newer, compressed rock we called "bedrock sandstone." (In our area, we have many outcroppings of Paleozoic sandstones dating back about 500 million years.) I pulled out a piece of local sandstone and asked, "Who wants to play the part of Bedrock?" I chose six or seven "Bedrocks," put signs on them, and asked these girls to huddle together on the ground. "When we start the play," I then explained, "Wind and Water will 'wave' and 'blow' through Bedrock, breaking it back into individual, 'unglued' sand particles."

Next, I asked someone to be Glacier. (Here in the Midwest, glaciers came through at various times in the last two million years, ripping up bedrock, grinding the pieces down, and carrying the soil-making material to our area. Some of the sand in our jar, I pointed out, may easily have come from hundreds of miles north.) Thus, Glacier, in our little drama, had the job of "crunching and grinding" and moving bedrock sand particles even more.

The rest of the girls, except one, were given signs representing small to microscopic animals (including moles, worms, mites, insect larvae, nematodes, and bacteria) and plants. As plants, they would fall on the ground, wriggle up, fall down, and wriggle up again and again in imitation of the cycles of plants growing, dying, and growing again.

At this point, we briefly returned to the jar of water and soil. I showed the plants that they would become the floating humus (decayed matter) on top, while the finer particles would be in the middle, and the broken up bedrock would end up as sand at the bottom of the jar.

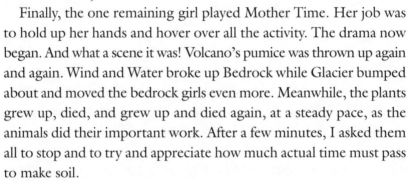

Finally, the one remaining girl played Mother Time. Her job was to hold up her hands and hover over all the activity. The drama now began. And what a scene it was! Volcano's pumice was thrown up again and again. Wind and Water broke up Bedrock while Glacier bumped about and moved the bedrock girls even more. Meanwhile, the plants grew up, died, and grew up and died again, at a steady pace, as the animals did their important work. After a few minutes, I asked them all to stop and to try and appreciate how much actual time must pass to make soil.

"Once bedrock is broken up, it takes approximately 500 years to make one inch of topsoil!"

"Let's now pretend that ten seconds is one hundred years of time," I said. "Everyone freeze and consider all the things that are happening. Mother Time will hold her hands over the scene, and we will call out every one hundred years (every ten seconds). Remember, nobody can move. You must simply think about everything going on."

"One hundred years . . . two hundred years . . . three hundred years . . ." Frozen kids. Each ten seconds seemed unbearably long. "Four hundred years . . . and finally five hundred years."

"And after all this work, here is what we have." I pulled a towel off a pie pan and on the bottom was one inch of soil. It was a grand achievement!

"But," I asked, "is it enough to grow a tree?"

"No."

"Could it grow a stalk of corn?"

"No."

A small seedling, at best, might grow in the soil we had. We would obviously have to make many, many inches to grow a tree.

While we were discussing this last point, a gust of wind (fortuitously) came through, creating an opportunity to demonstrate wind erosion. Picking up some soil from the pan, I let it blow out of my hands. I took another handful and blew on it this time, and that soil was gone, too.

I was now beginning to sense an element of frustration (even some anger) from the girls at what I was doing. All that work! All that time put into making our inch of topsoil, and now it was so easily, so quickly lost to the wind. We looked down at the pan. It was a depressing sight—spots of bare, polished aluminum. Now we couldn't even grow a small seedling.

We then walked over to a worn path that went down a bank to a creek. The trail was bare of vegetation and had begun to show signs of erosion. "Why is the path losing its soil?" I asked.

We noted that the vegetation, which contributes to the making of soil, is also important in keeping it from washing away, especially on a steep slope. I then put some of our homemade topsoil on the path and asked the girls where they thought it would eventually end up.

Obviously, the first hard rain would carry the soil into the creek below. We mentally followed its inevitable trip to the local Red Cedar River, to the Chippewa River and the Mississippi, and finally into the Gulf of Mexico. (Here it would have been helpful to have brought along a map of the United States.) Then, standing beside the stream, I once again asked them to remain quiet for a moment and to think about what we had learned in the past hour.

The long geological and biological processes of soil building plus the depressing feeling of losing soil to erosion; these were the things I wanted the girls to know, and especially to *feel*. Indeed, we should all feel the fragility of the topsoil from time to time. And from this knowledge, we will, hopefully, become more respectful and more vigilant in preserving the wonderful soil we still have—a resource so amazing, so precious, and as we witnessed this day, so very vulnerable, too.

CHAPTER 3

A Passion for Learning

Years ago, I wrote that many people in their worst night-mares find themselves once again a student in school. Since then many others have said the same. Many mature and competent adults tell me that to this day they feel uneasy in a school building, as if they were guilty of some crime, but didn't know what."

—JOHN HOLT

Is it, I wonder, possible to teach meadowlark values? Of course, some teachers make a great effort to encourage students to know and value local plants and animals and their amazing ecological relationships. Yet I wonder if they should aim for something slightly different, something beyond knowledge itself.

The purpose of teaching, in my view, is to instill a passion for learning. If teachers are doing their job, they will help their students acquire a lifetime love for learning itself, providing a long-term rather than short-term benefit. This is something students can use as they grow and mature, until the end of their days. If teachers don't somehow move their students toward this objective, even in a small way, I don't think the teachers can be considered completely successful.

15

Deep down, I have a feeling that nurturing a passion for learning should not be too difficult. The process of growing and becoming a more self-reliant learner, of prospecting for humankind's creations and discoveries, ought to be an exciting adventure full of delights and surprises that touch both heart and mind.

Yet as we all know, this is often not the case. Teachers with enthusiasm and the best of intentions frequently end up as mechanical dispensers of information and facts. Many feel that the only way they can overcome the students' resistance to learning is to force-feed them through coercion and fear.

Power and fear—these seem to be the tools most frequently used "to get the job done." What a frustration the entrenched use of these methods must be for a new teacher with high hopes and good intentions. And from the viewpoint of the students who recall the fun of learning new things on their own before schooling, and who wish to become persons of greater value later on in their lives, the situation is even worse. Such students must feel robbed. What was once an inner-directed drive for learning is now based on trying to please other people so that one can successfully "get through the system." For those who eventually want to become self-learners, undoing the damage is very difficult, if not impossible, like decontaminating radioactive substances.

Is there any hope for this unfortunate state of affairs? Under our current schooling system, the prospects appear dim, yet it is interesting to note the few cases in which these suffocating habits did not develop. For example, among the various teachers I have known, a few have been able to avoid these pitfalls. They did not succumb to the usual mechanical teaching. Instead, they retained their enthusiasm year after year, and what is even more amazing, they succeeded in instilling in their students a genuine excitement for learning—surely a meadowlark value if there ever was one. But what was their secret? What qualities did these memorable teachers have in common?

From my observations, they all seemed to have the following three characteristics: First, these teachers put a high priority on creating a positive attitude toward their subject matter, as opposed to the usual goal of simply imparting a certain body of knowledge. It's not that knowledge and facts are unimportant, but that information is used more as a vehicle to get students excited about the process of learning. Teachers can tell if they are on the right track by listening to their students. Such comments as "Boy, do I love economics!" or "Isn't biology (or _____) interesting?" demonstrate a healthy attitude, one that is a good indicator that self-learning is not far off.

The second ability of good teachers is the ability to relate other areas of knowledge into their own discipline and then to the students' own experiences and current levels of knowledge. This quality implies that the teacher herself is interested in diverse subjects and thus is a good model of self-learning.

I believe students often feel a certain disconnectedness as they travel from one box of knowledge to another. The sum often becomes less than the disconnected parts. Unfortunately the students rarely develop skills that will help them tie these seemingly disconnected parts together.

When a holistic integration is done expertly, as with the late Carl Sagan, Loren Eiseley, or Lewis Thomas, the performance can be breathtaking. Yet there seems to be little or no attempt in our schools, from kindergarten to graduate school, to cultivate these integrative skills or reward teachers who pursue them. Perhaps it is collegial pressures or simply ingrained teaching habits that make it so difficult to climb over the high walls of discipline specialization in our day-to-day dealings with students.

Let us assume that we can avoid the problems cited above. Assume too that we are able to retain, as teachers, an unusual degree of enthusiasm—and yet, we *still* find our students unhappy and resentful. It's a situation in which things ought to be OK, but instead we find resistance to change and growth; we simply have not awakened in our students their innate potential for learning. What's wrong? What have we missed?

This brings us to the third, and perhaps most difficult quality to attain, for it involves some decontamination on the part of the teachers themselves. The third quality that good teachers have is a high regard for the student. Actually, it's more than that. They clearly demonstrate a profound *respect* for their student's native intelligence and potential for discovery.

This means, for example, that teachers of physics would give the same respect, the same esteem, to each individual student that they might give to, say, the great geniuses of their discipline—to a young Marie Curie or Albert Einstein sitting in the classroom.

For many teachers, this third quality involves a radical rethinking of what education is all about. Indeed, we find no simple techniques that will help the teachers out on this one. But when respect is there, it is really there. The students know it. Respect is transmitted in a thousand little ways. It operates like a magic whirlpool that loosens up tight muscles of resistance and thaws cold fear.

When a teacher truly respects his or her students, their relationship is no longer one based on power but on equality. When a student says something impressive, the teacher is truly impressed and, indeed, might learn something new. The only real authority teachers have is some extra knowledge in an interesting or useful discipline, nothing more. Traditional authority and power have no place in the relationship.

In the end, respect brings respect, resulting in a situation in which students may actually realize these high expectations, often in surprising ways. Those few successful teachers know the truth of this. How did they learn it? Perhaps by trial and error, perhaps by instinct—I don't know. I wish I knew.

I do know that teachers who combine these three qualities—a positive attitude, integrated presentations, and a deep respect for their students—will, in their own small way, move their students closer to becoming self-reliant and sensitive learners. These students will be able to begin formulating a healthy set of values and also begin evolving meaningful personal philosophies, while gaining sufficient confidence to adapt to life's ever-changing problems. All these are fruits from teachers teaching one of the great goals of a lifetime—a passion for learning.

CHAPTER 4

High Jumping

*Of all the formulations of play, the briefest and the best
is to be found in Plato's Laws. He sees the model of true
playfulness in the need of all young creatures, animal
and human, to leap. To truly leap, you must learn how
to use the ground as a springboard, and how to land
resiliently and safely. It means to test the leeway allowed
by given limits; to outdo and yet not escape gravity.*

—ERIK ERICKSON

A long with healthy learning environments—nurturing our mind's passion to learn—"meadowlark values" imply healthy bodies. Doesn't the "animal within" whisper to us get up and away from the dull glare of our electronic screens, our pixeled universe, to flee from our seat-bound offices and commuter confinements, to *move*, to delight (like all critters) in multifarious motions, activities, and sundry skills?

Consider our urge to run, to launch or hit a ball, to dance away the night, or to execute a karate smack (or glide gently into T'ai Chi's Wave Hands like Clouds)—or simply to leap, to spring up and thereby test our body's many powers. Most of us have a favorite activity and a story to share; for me, I feel lucky to connect my athletic urge with family culture and my early education. It's a rather odd story that begins over a hundred years ago in the little town of Blue Mound, Illinois.

Family rumor has it that, somewhere, there's a photo of my grandfather as a young boy, high jumping in the backyard of his Blue Mound home. Someday, I'd like to see this picture, for it connects him with me. You see, I love to high jump, too.

In fact, jumping has been a minor passion of mine since grade school. Just about everywhere I have ever lived, I have constructed a set of crude high-jump standards and have somewhere located a suitable crossbar. That's pretty much all one needs, except for a soft place to land.

Before you get the wrong impression, however, I must confess right off that, despite my obsession with jumping, I'm not a very good jumper. Most high schoolers today who jump only as high as I do would probably not make the track and field team. Years ago, my young son asked me quite honestly if I was "approaching the world's record." (He'd like to be proud of his dad, if for no reason than to brag to his friends.) He soon learned the truth, as verified by his own copy of the *Guinness Book of World Records*, that his father jumps more than three feet below what the best jumpers can do. Not very impressive. If my memory is correct, I actually jumped higher in the ninth or tenth grade; but, even then, I never made the team.

I'm often haunted by the thought that if I had made the high-school team or had been forced to jump in a phys-ed class, I'd probably now have little, if any, interest in high jumping. I am intrigued, for example, by the late George Sheehan's question, "What happened to our play on our way to becoming adults?" and his answer is this:

Downgraded by the intellectuals, dismissed by the economists, put aside by the psychologists, it was left to the teachers to deliver the coup de grace. Physical education was born and turned what was joy into boredom, what was fun into drudgery, what was pleasure into work.[1]

One might speculate what other amateur enjoyments and later-life pleasures were also ruined by schooling.

It is not for achievement, honor, or record heights that I jump. I jump simply because I enjoy it. First, I enjoy thinking about the jump beforehand, then translating thought into action—slowly running toward the bar, speeding up on the last step or two, and in a flash, hurling myself over!

Sometimes I experiment with different speeds, different steps, different zones of concentration. Like any other sport, high jumping can be infinitely complicated or wonderfully simple. The pure analytical side is interesting; but more fun is the sense of abandon, of letting go. Of course, I have yet to feel anything grandiose. For me, there's been no Zen *satori*, no ecstasies to report. Yet, I can honestly say that, once or twice, I've actually felt like I was, well, *flying* (if only for an instant). It was not unlike that wonderful sensation I once felt, when young, in dreams. I've also been able to jump without thinking of anything in particular—just feeling connected to the environment and to the present moment—feet against dirt, wind and sun on my back, and at the same time, listening to the intermittent sound of crows, crickets (great jumpers themselves!), and off in the distance, hearing the call of a mourning dove. All the while, I have been loping toward the bar, when suddenly I spring, converting horizontal momentum into vertical flight.

To jump any reasonable height takes balance, rhythm, coordination, and good form. My jumping style is the old-fashioned Western Roll first perfected by Stanford jumper George Horne in 1912. It is a technique that takes more time to learn than the easy Scissors, or the simple Straddle (jumping as if you had tried to leap up onto a horse's back and wound up on the other side!) or even the backward leap common today called the "Fosbury Flop."

In jumping the Western Roll, you take off from your inside foot while kicking your outside foot as hard and as high as you can. As your kicking leg approaches the bar, your body and take-off leg quickly rise to join the upper leg so that everything rolls over pretty much at the same time. A photograph taken at the instant of clearance shows the jumper lying on his side, parallel to the bar, with the kicking leg stretched out and the take-off leg slightly tucked in near the bar. Unlike some of the other styles, such as the Scissors or Straddle (where one leg goes over first then the other), here everything goes over the bar simultaneously, thus enhancing the sensation of flying.

I was somewhat surprised to learn that no recent athlete has broken the world's high-jump record using this technique. But in 1912, Horne cleared six feet, seven inches (a record for his era), and more recently, Gene Johnson made a little over seven feet using the Roll. However, today's best jumpers, using the Fosbury Flop, are jumping eight feet or more!

Let me repeat that I jump because I like to jump. I've jumped in the rain, and I've jumped when there was snow on the ground. Sometimes, I'll jump when I don't feel very well. Often I've discovered that the way I jump tells me something about my physical or mental state. I've also discovered that high jumping can be an interesting exercise in learning to confront fear. Any time you jump at chest level or above, you're obviously taking some physical risk. There the metal bar sits—unwavering, inelastic, and uncompromisingly hard. The bar I currently use is triangular, made of an aluminum alloy, and has sharp edges. If my knee hits it, it can be quite painful. I've also sprained my jumping foot, and it is not unusual for me to hurt my back or wrist.

A good jump puts you many feet into the air, and, sooner or later, you must return to the earth. Yet, I've discovered that it's nearly impossible to make a satisfying jump when I have even the slightest air of caution about me. At the moment of take-off, I must surrender to an instantaneous intuition. A good jump, in short, involves a faith that everything will go perfectly, yet, a speck of fear often intrudes at the last moment, forcing me either to abort or make a miserable and often painful jump. (Could this be some kind of metaphor for life?)

So perhaps now you understand why I keep jumping. It's somehow wrapped up in the thrill of animal power, the skill of form, that light-hearted letting go, and, sometimes, the feeling of flight. Someday, it might even be more than that.

Why couldn't high jumping (or any other similar sport) evolve into a more mystical state, such as can be found in the martial arts of China or Japan? Why couldn't we experience, after sufficient skill development and concentration, something equivalent to what Eugen Herrigel describes in his book *Zen in the Art of Archery* as a state of

> *. . . serene pulsation which can be heightened into the feeling, otherwise experienced only in rare dreams, of extraordinary lightness, and in the rapturous certainty of being able to summon up energies in any direction.*[2]

It's surely something to look forward to. In the meantime, for me at least, I'll continue my unspectacular leaps, satisfied with the surprise of hearing the song of a meadowlark; with friendly crickets nearby, or thoughts of childhood and Grandpa Bauer jumping in Blue Mound, Illinois; with corn rustling in the garden, spruce nearby, grass bending in the wind, the sun disappearing behind a cloud, I pause, lope, run, kick, and I'm off!

CHAPTER 5

A Compensatory Ethic

One of the penalties of an ecological education is that
one lives alone in a world of wounds.

—ALDO LEOPOLD

Some fifty years ago, wildlife ecologist Aldo Leopold wove various ideas together into a memorable essay he called "The Land Ethic." To Leopold's credit, his land-ethic concept has become the centerpiece vision for ecologists, preservationists, and outdoors people alike. Indeed, I've seen no better definition of meadowlark values than can be found in Leopold's book *A Sand County Almanac.* In his essay, Leopold asserts that we are "members of a community of interdependent parts" and that it is time to consider enlarging the boundaries of that community to include not just humans, but plants, animals, soils, lakes, rivers, and oceans, or collectively—the *land.*

Recognition of this broader community carries with it a commitment of coexistence with and protection of all these diverse natural entities. In short, Leopold challenged us to begin rethinking the role of *Homo sapiens* from "conqueror of the land community to plain member or citizen of it."

"Plain member." I especially appreciate the word *plain*, a word that implies an uncharacteristic dose of humility and modesty. As we move away from the role of land conqueror, many now believe that we must begin to fairly share Earth's finite resources. This would imply a profound alteration of our industrial-based standard of living. In his vision, Leopold has begun to describe one of the ultimate goals of our species—a true transformation, on a large and permanent scale, of our public and private attitude toward the natural world— a goal even Leopold realized would take generations to accomplish.

In the meantime, what can be done? Are there any intermediate ethical stances we can use as stepping-stones along the way? Let me suggest one: a compensatory ethic. *Compensate* is defined as, "to make up for or to offset, counterbalance, to make equivalent or satisfactory reparation to. . . ."

A compensatory ethic would surely be less revolutionary than Leopold's land ethic. It would not insist that we immediately reduce our standard of living nor necessarily shun a practical level of material abundance. It does, however, imply that if we wish to continue with our resource-using, materialistic habits, we should somehow compensate or mitigate the damage by commitments to offset the negative consequences of our current level of production and consumption. An illustration of compensatory ethical action is a decision by a relatively small electrical utility—Applied Energy Services of Arlington, Virginia—to help finance the planting of fifty million trees in Guatemala. This investment is a good-faith commitment to compensate for the utility's annual carbon dioxide emissions by planting future carbon dioxide absorbers.

Along the same line, I wonder why countries with tropical rain forests have not made the following compensatory proposal to the developed countries: "OK industrial nations, if you want our forest diversity and also want to continue to enjoy the fruits of fossil fuels—but don't want the 'greenhouse' consequences—you can 'rent' our CO_2 absorbers and diverse animal and plant habitats." One way to raise the money would be to impose a CO_2 user tax on technologies and products (such as cars and electricity) that directly or indirectly burn fossil fuels. In addition, the subsidy could be used to foster the economic survival of traditional tropical populations who might otherwise be slashing and burning tracts of trees on relatively fragile forest topsoils.

If one accepts this line of argument and commits to exploring compensatory ethical options, a number of creative alternatives should pop into mind. A few years ago, for example, I passed by the site of a new Kmart store. Its enormous parking lot (then empty of cars) looked like a miniature blackened desert. I paced the lot's perimeter and found it to be roughly 134 by 143 steps, or approximately 19,000 square yards, a sizable area with no soils or animals—not even an exotic weed.

With such a sealing of the land, our compensatory ethic cries out for Kmart and its car-habituated customers (including myself) to make amends for suffocating the soil. Couldn't Kmart or the local shopping mall arrange to preserve a natural habitat—a rare forest grove, a remnant prairie, or a marshland perhaps? How about a contribution to the Nature Conservancy, an organization that has demonstrated expertise at this kind of thing?

It could be a modest investment that would simply reflect habitat gained for habitat lost. If voluntary contributions are not forthcoming, perhaps a paving tax would be in order to subsidize the protection of environmentally sensitive areas. Personally, I would feel much better about patronizing a Kmart store or a shopping center if I was assured that, in some way, they had "paid their dues," helping to preserve the natural world.

Compensatory ethics is a topic that's challenging to think about and also fun to discuss. Creativity, plus a little ecological understanding, is all that's needed to spin out a variety of compensatory strategies. Consider, for example, the ecological implications of deciding to have a child! How might one apply compensatory ethics to such a decision?

On a simpler level, let me ask a question. Do you burn wood? I do. I hereby pledge to plant as many trees as (or more trees than) I burn each year. This ethic is just common sense, and not much of a burden. I'm surprised how blind I've been to this true meadowlark value in my twenty-five years of burning wood. Furthermore, I will commit myself to compensate in other ways. Eventually I may opt for a simpler, less consumptive lifestyle and thereby reduce my compensatory debt.

So all you readers and businesspeople, what are your compensatory commitments? If we can make some headway with this and other ethical stepping-stones (while wending our way toward Aldo Leopold's land ethic), then our home planet, so pained and pummeled over the years, might spin with relief, as if knowing we were doing our best to restore and preserve her astonishing aliveness, diversity, and ever-surprising beauty.

CHAPTER 6

The Coming Repair Age

Great trouble comes
From not knowing what is enough.
Great conflict arises from wanting too much.

—LAO-TZU

Have you ever broken your glasses? No, not the lens, but that thin plastic section in the middle of the frame? Surely it happens to people now and then, for it recently happened to me. If your frames did break, did you try to repair them? Were you successful?

My broken glasses got me to thinking about the importance of mending skills, particularly in relation to our present and future economic situation. After considering the matter for a while, I came to the conclusion that we really should be putting more of our energies into the art of repair and maintenance.

It's no secret that, sooner or later, the world's energy supplies will dwindle, and that Earth's once large supply of raw materials will become increasingly scarce. Meadowlark values (and also just plain common sense) tell us that there simply must be an end to our wastefulness, that we cannot continue our gross consuming habits for the long run. There seem, in this respect, to be two fundamental choices: The first is simply "more of the same," continued economic growth and eventual economic collapse.

The second choice is to move toward a repair society, one that sustains itself on what we have today, with some opportunities for new and worthwhile inventions from time to time.

I hope we select the second alternative, to consciously *choose* to save those things that are useful and then keep them in sound working order for ourselves and posterity. This mode of living begins with an appreciation for the elegance of repair and the ritual of maintenance.

I began to understand this point more clearly while reading a lovely book, entitled *Craftsmen of Necessity*, by Christopher Williams. Consider the following quote:

> *The indigenous societies of the world gear their lives to a small assortment of deeply loved goods, gently made, carefully used and lovingly repaired.*[1]

When I first read this passage, I was reminded of a small Kikuyu stool I saw in Kenya. There was no doubt that this lovely artifact—with its circular, concave seat and gay (though somewhat distorted) faces on each of its three legs—was the work of a true craftsperson. But what I admired most was its exquisite repair work.

Small pieces of broken wood were carefully sewn together with thin copper wire, the ends of which were artfully coiled in patterns of concentric circles contrasting wonderfully with the dark stain of the smooth wood. Where breaks had to be bridged, there were short, flat lengths of scrap copper tightly binding the broken pieces. Magnificent!

Imagine somebody taking an interest in preserving this artifact over the years. These handsome repairs may have been made over a hundred years or more. I don't know.

I do know that the Gurungs, a traditional tribal community of central Nepal, have shown equal ingenuity. A repairer's reputation may well span generations:

> *The Gurung's compulsive resourcefulness is almost an embarrassment to the casual observer. Axes, ploughs and digging tools are used until they are worn beyond recognition. The village blacksmiths then reincarnate the stubs into another generation of tools and utensils; Aama can recall the lineage of successive incarnations of each of her pots, ladles and hoes. . . .*[2]

Traditional Resourcefulness

Do the above descriptions of ingenious improvisations, artful repair, and meticulous maintenance describe our future? I believe so, though surely we have a ways to go to match the Kikuyu or Gurung's art and skill of mending and maintenance. Yet, putting artfulness aside, some of us have made impressive progress when it comes to equaling their ingenuity.

I think, for example, of a farmer who lives down the road from us. Here's a man who, years ago, became annoyed when successive pick-up trucks inevitably began to rust and deteriorate. He noticed, however, that, where oil had collected on areas of the truck or other machinery, the machine's parts remained rust-free and workable. If the old oil was protecting paint, the enamel underneath was as shiny and colorful as the day he bought the machine. His conclusion? If he could discover a way to saturate all rustable areas of the truck with oil, he could keep it working well, perhaps forever. My friend had to find a method to spray oil into the furthest reaches of the truck's chassis. He would also need to coat the insides of doors, rocker panels, fender seams, the hollow of the tailgate, and all the bolts, springs, nuts, and screws.

Through trial and error, he finally developed a surprisingly efficient spraying device out of a junked oil-filter canister from a twenty-five-year-old Chevy; it's a simple improvisation that delivered vaporized oil to all points in and around the vulnerable parts of the truck. He had to drill holes and do other ingenious things to get the correct mixture of air and oil. He then snapped the contraption onto his air compressor, attached a long hose with a tiny trigger-operated nozzle, and he was finally in business.

My friend once asked me to carefully examine his sixteen-year-old Ford truck, to see if I could find any rust breaking through. I looked and looked and looked. There was none. Believe me, I was impressed. And he accomplished this feat with discarded parts and waste oil. He now owned a truck that, with infrequent oilings, he could perhaps pass on to another generation—a Gurung at heart!

Another neighbor of mine has successfully nursed along a thirty-year-old hay baler. He knows everything about it—everything. He can make virtually any repair without fear or befuddlement.

I also know someone who "repairs" old prairie remnants, defining his work in terms of restoring, or "healing," native natural areas. He too loves the various rituals of repair and maintenance, including—among other things—setting prairie fires in the spring.

These are just a few examples of the harbingers of a new maintenance ethic, prophets of the coming repair age.

Incidentally, I did surprise myself when I finally fixed my broken glasses frame (with one of those superglues). But it wasn't particularly elegant, nothing like the mending of the stool, or as beautiful as restored prairie grasses and prairie flowers waving in the wind.

Most of us need additional skills to practice this meadowlark value, the art of healing, repair, and maintenance—a seemingly lost art in our fast-paced, consumer society. It will surely be something new for us, we who are so accustomed to our wasteful and destructive ways, or we might look at the future repair age as simply "coming home again," arriving safely after the big party.

CHAPTER 7

An Ideal Boss

Where other companies speak of a supervisor or fore-man, IBM speaks of an assistant. . . . He is to be the "assistant" to his workers. His job is to be sure that they know their work and have tools. He is not their boss.

—PETER DRUCKER

As we explore the values of holistic economics, we might want to take a moment to consider the elements of an effective worker/supervisor relationship. If you are like me, you've probably asked yourself that simple but important question: What are the qualifications for an ideal boss? This individual might be a supervisor in a business, the armed forces, or perhaps in a university or government agency.

Yet, in my own opinion, the common terms *boss* and *supervisor* may carry the wrong message. By implying that it's necessary for workers to be "bossed" or "supervised" by a superior, both terms begin with the assumption of some degree of worker incompetence. My preference would be to use the word *administrator* instead—a designation less hierarchical, more plastic, and therefore more open to creative interpretation than "boss" or "supervisor."

What then should our model administrator do or not do? What are his or her functions within the organization, and how does this person differ from the traditional "bosses" of today? Undoubtedly every business writer has his or her own list of skills and competencies needed to become the so-called "effective manager." For my own ideal administrator, however, let me suggest four functions.

Gardener

I use this term because gardeners, especially organic gardeners, see their present activity in terms of the long run. Good gardeners prepare their soil for years ahead. Aware of long nutrient cycles, gardeners begin gathering materials now, in the form of old hay, kitchen scraps, and manure, to make compost that may not break down for a year or two. Once the compost is added to the soil, the gardener may not see results until much later. With this perspective, gardeners tend to be optimists; they are convinced that small decisions today will add considerable quality to the enterprise many years hence.

In addition, gardeners seem to enjoy the art of experimenting, and they don't seem to get upset if projects sometimes fail. They're anxious to try new varieties, different ways of planting, and novel ways to build up topsoil—things that add interest and excitement and offer the experimenter something to look forward to.

Now, the administrator as gardener views his or her operating unit in a similar way, with the goal being the long-term success of the enterprise and the well-being of the workers. The administrator should offer encouragement, praise, and opportunities for individual development, knowing that these actions may not have a payoff immediately but will surely nurture happier, more loyal, and more productive workers for the long run.

Using the gardener as a model, the administrator should also encourage experimentation and expect some failure, for this is what makes the job interesting and creates possibilities for true innovation. This particular role is the administrator's most satisfying, for it offers the greatest potential for making lasting improvements.

Intervener

Of the four functions, this one comes closest to the conventional boss. The head of a unit must communicate the larger objectives or missions of the organization to the workers. Combined with this duty, he or she also has the responsibility to intervene in those cases in which a worker disregards the goals or the specific policies of the hierarchy. Judgments must be made quickly when such behavior seems likely to threaten the reputation or effectiveness of the unit. Nothing is more demoralizing to the rank-and-file staff than the times when those outside of the work unit begin to view the group with diminishing esteem, particularly when the problem lies with one or two individuals. Such problem behavior is often brought to a halt by one's coworkers, but when they fail, the administrator must intervene or the end result may well be more control and regimentation imposed by the hierarchy.

This kind of intervention involves an immense amount of tact, plus an ability to criticize and persuade the individual to change his or her actions without permanently damaging the worker's sense of self-worth. If the one-to-one intervention does not work, then the administrator must sound out the staff for their suggestions for handling the situation. In extreme cases, perhaps psychiatric help is in order. As a last resort, the administrator may have no choice but to fire the worker. Whatever the solution, the administrator must know how to handle this delicate situation with skilled diplomacy. It is not an easy job.

Resource Person

The third function of our ideal administrator is that of resource person. Many conventional supervisors may find this function or skill the most difficult to learn. For a good model, let me suggest one that, though unusual today, was once common in the medical industry: a hospital administrator's relationship to the doctors.

In these settings, the administrator is usually not the boss, but more a servant. The administrator regards the doctors as professionals who know best how to do what they are doing. The administrator is hired to take care of the patients' records, billing, marketing, and other details the doctors do not have time for if they are to be good at their specialties. A good administrator in this role ought to be visiting various departments, asking questions such as "What can I do for you?" or "How might I make your job easier?" Although this approach may sound logical, how often do we hear such kind and helpful words from our supervisors?

The main thing to keep in mind is that the administrator should always regard his or her individual staff members as experts in their respective fields who, from time to time, will need extra services or resources that only someone in an administrative position can provide. I see no reason why this idea cannot be applied in the executive suites of General Motors; in the administration of a university, the army, or government department; or even between worker and foreman on an assembly line.

Lobbyist

In almost all large organizations, departments and divisions compete for scarce resources. These resources are usually thought of in terms of money and staffing, but they might also include other benefits, such as the quality of the workplace, access to policy making, flexibility, and other tangibles and intangibles that are conferred by the hierarchy.

Therefore, an administrator should learn a little of the art of politics and public relations. There will be times when the lobbyist role demands even more than the usual political representation, especially when the survival of the unit is in question. On such occasions, an administrator should know how to negotiate effectively, to defend with skill and determination the vital interests of the department. He or she must know how to deal with subtle power plays of others who may be out to destroy. In such times, good administrators must convince the hierarchy that their workers are not only making short-term contributions to the larger organization but are working toward long-term objectives as well.

Of course, this kind of political activity can be an especially unpleasant business. Administrators may feel it necessary to make friends with people they do not particularly like. They may have to advertise their department's virtues and minimize its faults.

Unfortunately, many individuals in this role feel the need to overlook illegalities such as bribes, kickbacks, and padded expense accounts; they might lie about ineffective or dangerous products or (in violation of meadowlark values) poison the environment.

Indeed, such unethical actions may catch up with the person in question—first on a personal, moral basis, next within the organization and, finally, publicly. When this happens, they jeopardize the morale and possibly even the survival of the entire department, those things that had taken the administrator years to build up as a resource person or gardener. When an administrator engages in such questionable activities, it is essential that the people within the unit act as interveners—at first, privately, then publicly if necessary.

Nevertheless, the ideal administrator must, at times, be realistic about power relationships within the organization; they must aggressively defend their department against encroachments and sometimes make the necessary compromises that can and do take place in any "political" arena.

Still, if the lobbyist function is performed well, there can be no better payoff than to have the staff respect their administrator. Simple respect will ultimately make the other roles of resource person, intervener, and gardener much easier and thereby fostering the deeper (meadowlark) values of health, growth, and well-being for workers, administrators, and the organization itself.

CHAPTER 8

Craftsmanship and Salvation

After a long time, I felt that I had to choose one way of living or the other. . . . I took heart again in the old ways and did what my father had told me to do, carve monuments to my people, small monuments. And then my life changed. A new spirit came back into me and my life became so great that the sky could not cover it, the mountains and forests of home could not contain it and the wind and rivers could not move it."
—GERARD RANCOURT TSONAKWA

For some years now, I have had a values argument with my father. He believes that we all move forward by enlarging our individual and collective productivity. He tells me that we must grow "two blades of grass where only one grew before." Efficiency and productivity, he says, have not only given us our present high standard of living but will also be the forces driving us toward a better future. What are the tools that will bring this about? "More investment and better technology" is his answer.

I have always felt that, though his position was logically correct, something was intuitively wrong with his argument, but I was never quite able to put my finger on it. After all, isn't it better to drive into town than to walk? And why does one use a word processor instead of a pencil or pen and ink? My intuitive conviction that something was wrong fell apart when I observed my own behavior.

Craftsmanship Fosters Reverence

Now I believe I know what has been troubling me all these years. Modern machinery, technology, and the "cult of efficiency" destroys our age-old cultural need to engage periodically in slow-paced, traditional, craftsmanship.

When I speak of craftsmanship, I am not referring to the common complaint today that many of our products are shoddy and poorly designed, though to some degree this is true. Craftsmanship involves more than that. To me, craftsmanship implies a particular *attitude* toward the shaping of raw materials, and the final product, I think, is really secondary.

Though outwardly inefficient, inwardly a craftsperson gains a sense of satisfaction through their deep reverence for raw materials and tools skillfully used. W. H. Auden once wrote that if a person came to him and said, "I have important things to say," he or she would not likely become a poet. But if they said: "I feel like hanging around words, listening to what they say,"[1] then Auden felt that this person had a chance.

The craftsworker in glass savors glass and the furniture craftsworker loves wood. It's much like a love affair in which the craftsperson ultimately gives birth to some fine work or artifact. Sometimes the process is sensuous, and, at other times, the worker becomes so totally absorbed that the "self" is forgotten for a moment. It is perhaps something like a child intensively concentrating on play; at other times it may be more like a spiritual experience.

Indeed, most craftspeople whom I have known feel that there is a sacred quality to their work, that the activity takes place not in a conventional work environment but in more of a sanctuary. Years ago, Minnesota novelist Robert Pirsig described the process of tuning up a motorcycle:

The first tappet is right on, no adjustment required, so I move on to the next. . . . I always feel like I'm in church when I do this. . . . The gauge is some kind of religious icon and I'm performing a holy rite with it.[2]

Elsewhere in his book (*Zen and the Art of Motorcycle Maintenance*), Pirsig implies that motorcycle maintenance can be an art that can lead to an experience akin to Zen, where all existence is focused upon the moment, where the pain of the past and the anxieties of the future are dissolved as the worker becomes one with the work.

Now consider your friends and relatives. How many true craftsworkers do you know? Why are there so few? And why hasn't modern technology—especially the widespread use of computers—given us that broad margin of leisure time to pursue quality crafts? Though I certainly don't know all the reasons, I do know that when we make an obsession out of efficiency and technology, we are more likely to diminish our respect for any process that appears to be "inefficient." Furthermore, our high standard of living has given us so many choices that we seem compelled to consume each and every variety of experience available to us. "Efficient use of time" is the order of the day.

Yet, deep down, I suspect that many of us regret the loss of craftsmanship. I feel confident in saying this because I observe that people respond with genuine awe when they see a piece of work from the hands of a true craftsperson, such as handmade furniture, blown glass, a beautiful quilt, or a well-crafted poem. We read with envy and respect about the craftspeople of Appalachia, preservers of blacksmithing, herbal gathering, stone masonry, and the making of musical instruments, just to name a few. We know that somewhere, sometime we too would like to return to this world of relaxed pace, of deliberateness, and of carefully created forms that reflect what Pirsig called "Quality."

Perhaps what we are really seeking is a kind of salvation. Recall that Thoreau, in his final chapter of *Walden*, suggested that the true craftsman will never die. Our technocrats and ministers of efficiency would do well to remember Thoreau's account of the Kouroo artist who strove for perfection in the carving of a walking staff. After many years of working on the staff with endless love, patience, and complete absorption, he found that "his singleness of purpose and resolution . . . endowed him . . . with perennial youth." His friends died, dynasties came and went, and even the polestar changed position. Then at last, when he finally completed his task, the staff "suddenly expanded before the eyes of the astonished artist into the fairest of all creations of Brahma."

He had made a new system in making a staff, a world with full and fair proportions in which, though the old cities and dynasties had passed away and fairer and more glorious ones had taken their places, the material was pure, and his art was pure. How could the result be other than wonderful?[3]

CHAPTER 9

Simplify, Simplify: Henry Thoreau as Economic Prophet

> *Why should we be in such desperate haste to succeed and in such desperate enterprises? If a man does not keep pace with his companions, perhaps it is because he hears a different drummer. Let him step to the music which he hears, however measured or far away.*
>
> —HENRY THOREAU

Henry Thoreau, the nineteenth-century writer and naturalist, may have been one of the first to evolve a philosophy of "meadowlark values" in the field of economics. In fact, as a professional economist, I have became more and more convinced that this early American thinker is truly a prophet for our time, worthy of the ranks of the major economic philosophers such as Adam Smith, David Hume, and Thomas Malthus. Let's now take a moment to explore some of his ideas a little closer.

The Problem of Overabundance

Let's begin with the "farm crisis" of the late 1990s. Although agriculture has always had its ups and downs, the farmer who overexpanded, who acquired too much machinery, too much land, and in general incurred too much debt, is facing an especially demoralizing situation today: Farmers are incurring losses year after year, and they are finding it difficult, if not impossible, to get rid of their holdings. Though Thoreau did not specifically predict our contemporary farmers' dilemma, he did make a generic observation that seems wonderfully relevant to the situation. Thoreau warned us of the problem of overabundance and that our possessions can at times "be more easily acquired than got rid of." In the following passage from *Walden*, change the image slightly and see how Thoreau's vision has a surprisingly contemporary ring to it:

> *How many a poor immortal soul have I met well-nigh crushed and smothered under its load, creeping down the road of life, pushing before it a barn seventy-five feet by forty, its Augean stables never cleansed. . . .*[1]

Thoreau had sympathy for those who had too much, whose overabundance in their lives was more of a problem than a solution.

But if material possessions do not represent "the good life," what does? Might it come from the advance of technological conveniences? No doubt Thoreau marveled at, and benefited from, many of the by-products of the industrial revolution. He admitted to the advantages of shingles, boards, bricks, and especially glass window panes ("doorways of light . . . like solidified air!"[2]) in the construction of homes. Once he purchased a small telescope to better observe the birds. Also, as a part-time surveyor and pencil maker, he undoubtedly valued the various tools of these different professions. But, for the most part, Thoreau felt that inventions tended to be nothing more than "improved means to an unimproved end"[3] or "pretty toys which distract our attention from serious things."[4] At worst, a particular technology could be profoundly destructive to life itself. Consider, for example, this famous quote:

> *. . . but though a crowd rushes to the depot, and the conductor shouts "All Aboard" when the smoke is blown away, and the vapor condensed, it will be perceived that a few are riding, but the rest are run over.*[5]

"Run over." A strange statement. But not so out of place when we consider the many men, women, and children who are killed in transportation accidents. And if Thoreau wrote these words metaphorically (as I believe he did), who cannot recognize the rather chilling prophesy when one considers the total death and destruction possible with high-tech warfare or a catastrophic leak at a chemical factory or a nuclear power plant meltdown?

Or consider the giant machines that are used to devour hundreds of square miles of landscape in the pursuit of minerals and trees, or to prepare vast acres of good farmland for roads and suburban developments.

This kind of economic "progress," which ravages the environment, would have been especially distressing to Thoreau because he profoundly believed that there simply could not be a "good life," or even a completely healthy life, without access to nature:

> *There can be no very black melancholy to him who lives in the midst of nature and has his senses still.*[6]

And in his chapter "Spring," in *Walden*, he writes:

> *We need the tonic of wildness—to wade sometimes in marshes where the bittern and the meadow-hen lurk, and hear the booming of the snipe; to smell the whispering sedge where only some wilder and more solitary fowl builds her nest, and the mink crawls with its belly close to the ground.*[7]

Wilderness as Preservation of the World

Picture now this young man of thirty-four, standing before the Concord Lyceum in the spring of 1851 and opening his lecture with, "I wish to speak a word for Nature, for absolute freedom and wildness," and ending his lecture with the oft-quoted phrase: ". . . in wildness is the preservation of the world."[8]

His audience must have found these very strange words since an immense area of pure wilderness still existed in North America at that time. It's different now. Today it is not so difficult for us to understand Thoreau's passion for wilderness values and for the preservation of wild spaces as a prophetic idea, for us and for his New England audience of over a hundred years ago.

Henry Thoreau wished we might value our natural environment and work hard to preserve it against inevitable encroachments. But what else did Thoreau advocate? What did he specifically recommend individuals do to help themselves in their private lives? His answer was as profound as it was brief: "simplify, simplify!"[9] In an exaggerated moment, he advised his readers to "keep your accounts on your thumb-nail."[10] More realistically, Thoreau advocated that we reduce our economic needs, that is, engage in a kind of "voluntary poverty."[11] His greatest skill, he once remarked, has been "to want but little."[12] Another prophetic notion? Perhaps so, especially when we consider that, sooner or later, the industrialized countries will be forced into life patterns that require less use of energy and natural resources.

Reexamining Our Basic Values

If Thoreau were alive today, he would be appalled by our tremendous private and public debt, our growing dependence on government and the myriad specialists who reduce our capability to do important things for ourselves, and he would be advocating greater local economic independence—as much as was practical. He once suggested that we might learn to grow our own food, as well as build our own homes. For recreation, instead of our costly pre-packaged commercial experiences (going shopping, watching a video, visiting

Disneyland, etc.), Thoreau would advocate, among other things, simply taking a walk (as he did almost every day), launching oneself in the spirit of great adventure. Thoreau, according to his *Journal*, would not only be entertained and educated by his walks, but would also discover meaning and beauty on such "sauntering excursions" into and through the natural world within a few miles of his home.

If, in these and other ways, we would become more self-reliant, as our Concord economist suggested, wouldn't one's "stagnant income" lose some of its sting, the threat of inflation lose some of its terror? Wouldn't our feverish anxiety over economic growth diminish? And, in general, wouldn't life itself be more pleasant if we could slow down and become a little less serious in our striving for high material comfort? Thoreau honestly felt that, with some modest readjustment in our values and our expectations, we might view human existence in a much different, more positive light:

> *In short, I am convinced, both by faith and experience, that to maintain one's self on this earth is not a hardship but a pastime, if we will live simply and wisely. . . .*[13]

Thoreau, as economic prophet, asks us to reexamine our basic economic premises. Our traditional goal of high material consumption may well carry with it an unexpected price tag in the form of unpleasant complexities, stress, and anxieties. Thoreau's main objective would stress, instead be freedom, or, better yet, what he simply called *life*: "The cost of a thing is the amount of what I will call life which is required to be exchanged for it immediately or in the long run."[14]

For many contemporary economists and business people, this is indeed an odd theory of wealth, but it is one that is consistent with meadowlark values, one that Thoreau would defend both in his writings and in the way he lived. It is an idea that would force us all to look at our own lives and the larger economy in a slightly different perspective: GDP per capita would not be as important as something like *life* per capita, if that could somehow be measured.

Thoreau was genuinely concerned for the economic welfare of his fellow citizens. But he did not want us to waste our lives pursuing overabundance. He profoundly wished that we deepen ourselves—and take the necessary time to learn about and appreciate our amazing planetary wonders—and *not* wake up one morning, late in life, only to discover that we had never really lived.

PART TWO

Meadowlark Meditations
Celebrating Our Cosmic Journey

*To be alive is a miracle. To be alive and know that you
are alive is the greatest of all miracles.*
— THICH NHAT HANH

Leaving behind the economic philosophy of Henry Thoreau for a moment, we now move ahead—keeping in mind our imperative to go beyond the confines of economics and the issues of education, work, and consumption. This new perspective must include an evolutionary context to help us better understand and evaluate our unique place within the long sweep of our cosmological, biological, and cultural histories.

For me, this new, broader perspective adds a liberating dimension, one that leads toward a feeling of celebration and a sense of gratefulness regarding my own origins and my evolutionary connection to the other creatures on our planet. In addition, it will supply a new framework to ponder our place in the universe and explore human possibilities—a timely topic as we all prepare to gingerly step over into the next millennium. The topics of interest include astronomy, geology, anthropology, religion, and, of course, biological evolution through natural selection.

Before we commence with such a wide-ranging expedition through vast geological periods and astronomical spaces, let's pause for a moment—teetering between the subjects of economics and evolution—and attempt to bridge these two worlds.

Years ago, a student asked me to explain, if I could, the idea of evolution: "How does it work, and what does it mean?" she asked. (I believe I detected in her question elements of doubt and fear.) Furthermore, she asked me to explain Darwinian natural selection.

As an economist, I thought it might be interesting to compare market-based economics through the inner workings of biological evolution. Surely both systems share elements of common ground, although in other aspects they may be quite different. Consider two very interesting evolutionary creations, Ford's Mustangs and Darwin's finches, and let's investigate how each relates to the powerful forces of variation and the universal struggle of the survival of the fittest.

CHAPTER 10

Darwin's Finches and Ford's Mustangs

The lucky individual that finds a different seed, or nook, or niche, will fly up and out from beneath the Sisyphean rock of competition. It will tend to flourish and so will its descendants—that is, those that inherit the lucky character that had set it a little apart. . . .

—JONATHAN WEINER

"Survival of the fittest"—consider the many times we've heard this famous expression as applied to the business world. Other "Darwinian" phrases include "finding a niche" in the marketplace, "the struggle for existence," or the "extinction" of a company or of a product line. How easily the ideas and vocabulary of evolutionary biology seem to flow freely and interchangeably into the world of business and back again.

But how accurate is this analogy? Is Darwin's world of successful evolution by natural selection a workable metaphor for a business creating profitable product "variations" in the marketplace?

In one important sense—the method of creating variations—the analogy's a poor one. Why? Because Darwinian natural selection implies ongoing random variations of living organisms. In contrast, businesses develop products through *artificial selection*, through conscious and deliberate decisions on the parts of managers, designers, and engineers.

The Beak of the Finch

Nature, more often than not, uses a "shotgun" approach, "inefficiently" producing a large number of offspring, with some having an advantageous trait that improves their chances of survival. A good book describing this process is Jonathan Weiner's Pulitzer Prize-winning *The Beak of the Finch*. In it, the author weaves a fascinating story out of the long-term studies of the so-called "Darwin's finches" that survive on the Galapagos Islands off the coast of Ecuador.

These studies suggest that it is relatively small variations—say in the depth or length of a finch's beak—that can make the difference (especially in times of environmental stress) between the life and death of an individual bird. Favored birds, in turn, not only survive but will be more likely to successfully reproduce and pass their genes on to the next generation.

If Darwinian dynamics were literally applied to business, an automobile company would have to manufacture thousands of slightly different models each year, in the hope that one or a few might survive in the marketplace. Such a process would obviously be inefficient and highly unprofitable.

Businesses must condense their selection processes by artificially preselecting good designs, then testing them in advance with a sample of buyers. Today's automakers utilize 3-D computer modeling techniques to search for potentially marketable designs from virtually millions of possibilities. Indeed, why manufacture (as nature does) inefficient variations when they can be winnowed in advance using intelligent design and scientific market research techniques?

However, once the selection process has narrowed the possibilities, then a business/biology analogy becomes more accurate. For example, if a company's product becomes successful, it attracts sufficient "resources" (revenues and profits) to keep it "alive," thereby guaranteeing its "reproduction" (continued manufacture) until there's a change in the "environment" (consumer preferences, demographic changes, manufacturing costs, competition, etc.).

Edsels and Mustangs*

The parallels between nature and manufacture were highlighted some thirty years ago in Ford's epic Edsel failure, when compared with Ford's Mustang success. Edsel's development utilized no effective market research in the testing of stylistic variations. Although Ford put Edsel into a respectable niche occupied by Olds, Pontiac, and Buick, Edsel projected a poor front-end design, and early models also suffered from substandard mechanical quality. Edsel's developers made the unforgivable mistake of offering a new and relatively untested push-button gearshift mechanism that was costly to produce and suffered from an unacceptably high failure rate—near fifty percent in the first three months of sales! One could easily have predicted that, sooner or later, the "species" *Fordus edselus* would soon become "extinct."

In contrast, Mustang is still alive in the marketplace, projecting its familiar "morphology" (general body shape) through various transitional forms, up to and including the Mustang of today. Both Mustang's name and styling had the advantage of market research, starting with demographic studies that forecast a bulge of relatively young car buyers (post-war baby-boomers) ready to purchase their first car. (A biologist might say that a new and viable niche was emerging.)

For Ford, improved quality control also would be a consideration. High reliability would be important not just for the new model but as a selling point in the used-car market, a key factor in maintaining consumer brand loyalty.

In addition, the well-known name—Mustang—was chosen via a carefully planned and deliberate selection process. In the spring of 1963, Ford tested some thirty-three names. Survey groups were then asked

---

* I am indebted to my father, Robert Eggert, for his help in researching, reviewing, and editing this essay. Robert Eggert was Ford's market research manager from 1951–68.

to rate each name by two criteria: "suitability as a name for the special car" and a more generalized "feeling for the name" while viewing a photograph of the clay model.

In looking over the original results, the least popular names were Carnelliann, Calli, and Fangio. Lee Iacocca, then vice president of Ford Division, pushed for Turino, a name that scored slightly below average in both criteria. The name Thunderbird II did better, but not nearly as well as Panther, Dolphin, and Commando. Mustang (a name derived from the title of J. Frank Dobie's western novel *The Mustangs*) scored the highest.

How did the Mustang (in contrast to Edsel) keep quality up and prices down? Here we can see another analogy to Darwinian evolution. Consider again Darwin's famous finches: Studies suggest that the finch's evolutionary path takes place somewhat conservatively. Its underlying body (the "chassis") doesn't change very much. Although variations take place throughout the entire body over many generations, there's little selective pressure to change the basics. Variations in the beak appear to be the deciding factor in survivability, especially during periods of environmental stress.

In other words, the finch's basic "infrastructure" tends to be relatively reliable and therefore needs little alteration over time. So how does this idea relate to the Mustang? On this particular point, Ford had an evolutionary insight. In a critical decision in 1962, Mustang's development team made a decision to use the relatively reliable chassis and drive train of an earlier Ford model (the Falcon). Evolutionists might therefore call the Falcon a common ancestor to the Mustang, as well as subsequent Ford models built on the Falcon chassis. The upshot was that the Mustang's base price could be kept relatively low, an attractive $2,265. The car would also eventually earn an enviable reputation for reliability, since any bugs, common in brand-new models, had already been corrected.

It's intriguing to see how the title of a relatively obscure Western novel helped one giant automaker go from a walk to a gallop, and thereby make a profitable run across the sixties' economic landscape. Today, the famous '64 Mustang is the common ancestor of later Mustangs, having "speciated" into new niches, then radiated out into the various branches of an evolutionary tree . . . onward and upward toward Ford's Pinto, Bronco, and beyond!

Summary

From bird beaks to body styles, to our own evolutionary journey through time, we live in a wonderful world of creative change, energized by forces of natural and artificial selection forces, forces that brought us Earth's rainbow of diversity: amazing plants, astonishing animals, cultural adaptations, plus the relatively recent emergence of economic and technological artifacts of novelty, comfort, and modern-day survival.

In recognizing the creative potential of these forces, we are now in a position to briefly explore some of the interesting issues of our age: questions about our own evolutionary origins and also about where we might go from here—culturally, economically, and technologically.

Thus, as we once again listen to the song of the meadowlark, important questions come to the fore: What is our music? What is our (the human) role within the evolutionary scheme of things? Among other things, the following essays will take us back in time to explore the broad sweep of our cosmic and biological evolution. This investigation will provide a context to address more philosophical questions of our species' place, purpose, and unique possibilities.

CHAPTER 11

A Cosmic Journey

*Why should I feel lonely? Is not our planet in the
Milky Way?*

—Henry Thoreau

*There is that in me . . . it is without name . . . it is a
word unsaid. . . .
Something it swings on more than the earth I
swing on.
To it the creation is the friend whose embracing
awakens me.*

—Walt Whitman

Who are we? Where did we come from? And what does it mean
to be human? My own musings on these matters began in the
dark of night. I recall a mild summer evening years ago when my nine-
year-old daughter and I walked hand-in-hand to the back of our prop-
erty. On that unusually dark and beautiful night, we made our way
to a secluded part of our two acres.

Earlier, I had set up a small telescope in a relatively flat, unobstructed viewing area. We pointed our telescope toward the lovely constellation of Lyra, the "Harp" configuration of stars between the constellations of Cygnus and Hercules.[1]

Ring Nebula

We then took a peek at Lyra's unusual ring nebula, a donutlike gray-green wisp of fluorescence or, some might say, a faint puff of smoke from some far-off pipe. What we saw was actually a dying star twenty-two hundred light years away. Astronomers tell us that Lyra's ring is a bubble of hot gas expanding ever outward—a gentle, but final, shrug of a relatively small star that was once much like our own sun. We were, in a sense, witnessing a grand preview of our own stellar future.

Of course, our Sun's solar swelling and super heated ring-puff will happen five *billion* years from now—plenty of time for good digestion, a long life, plus sufficient geological eras for millions of future generations. But eventually our home star will evolve into what astronomers call a "red giant." It will swell and burn with intensity. Its expanding heat and searing bubble will burn Earth's precious skin of green and atmospheric blue. The heat will vaporize rivers and oceans alike, boil away every stream and splash of puddle.

"But," my daughter asked when I told her this, "Will people be able to live? Would we have to wear space suits? Could we move to Pluto?"

I was impressed with her strategies for survival. It may be possible to extend life on another planet or on a space station, but sooner or later, our Sun's hot ring and its inevitable burn out will leave scant hope for life-forms within this planetary neighborhood. Eventually,

> *. . . the Sun will be a cold, black-dwarf governing a retinue of fused and hard-frozen worlds orbiting in a darkness lit only by the light of the distant stars.*[2]

In the meantime, what do we do? One thing perhaps: Share the beauty, share the evening's all-aroundedness. Witness the moment, *this* moment. That night my daughter and I chatted about our feelings and about life's meanings. We mixed into our hour some science and silence while experiencing the deepening darkness and relishing the night's enchantment. Also, that August evening, we saw some

meteors. My companion counted eleven. Excitedly she nudged me—
"Look, look!"

As we packed up our telescope, we made a date to go out again.
But next time we would not observe star destruction, but stellar creation.
We promised each other that, come winter, we would take a peek at
Orion's famous nebula, a zone of the night sky that astronomers have
described as a "stellar nursery." In observing Orion's bright gas and
dust cloud, one can actually witness infant stars in the making, baby
stars sparkling through the blue-green glow of Orion's galactic mist.[3]
Such are some of the ongoing creations of our ever-evolving universe.

My daughter and I took one last glance overhead—taking in the
unearthly stillness and admiring the dark and deepening beauty.
Who, I wondered, has not sensed the larger questions as he or she
stood, so small, so insignificant, under the sweep of stars and the mystery of the night?

If I could, I would like to discover where we came from, to follow respectfully the old trail of universal history and visit, if I can,
some of the great landmarks of our intimate family history. Ideally,
I would like to make familiar the cosmic/biological sequences that
brought us to this moment of consciousness, to invite this universal
history into the mind and heart, not with fearful strangeness but with
understanding and affection, to make it as familiar as C.S. Lewis's
"soft slippers, old cloths, old jokes, and the thump of a sleepy dog's
tail on the kitchen floor."[4]

Emptiness

What actually happened then, in the interval from the original emptiness to this very moment—you sharing these thoughts and medita-
tions, or me sitting at my desk tapping at the keys of an old Royal
typewriter while enjoying the distant trill of a resident field sparrow?

Modern science and many cultures believe that there was a pause,
a silence. It might help to try and imagine pure space, pure emptiness. There are actually zones in our night sky where there's practically nothing at all: "Cosmic voids" they're called. Two voids that
have been closely studied are the Boötes Void (named after the

constellation that depicts a mythological herder) and the one in Coma Berenices ("The hair of Berenice"). You might try to find these constellations on some dark night in the spring. Then relax (take your time) and imagine the great gaps within them. Can you somehow feel the pure space and great emptiness of the pre-universe beginnings?

To get into the mood, I sometimes look through our telescope at an "empty" zone of the night sky away from the great masses of stars. For me, at least, this is a starting place. I look and look and look, taking in the magnified circle of magnificent blackness. On these special nights I recall the quotation from the *Tao Te Ching*, the Chinese philosophical/mystical book written in the fourth century B.C. by Lao-tzu:

> *The Way is a void/Used but never filled;/An abyss it is, /Like an ancestor/From which all things come. . . ,/ Whose offspring it may be/I do not know;/It is like a preface to God.*[5]

Looking out into the depths of space, within the ring of ultrablackness, one can sense the quiet:

> *There is a being, wonderful, perfect;/It existed before heaven and earth./How quiet it is! How spiritual it is! It stands alone and does not change,/It moves around and around but does not on this account suffer./All life comes from it./It wraps everything with its love as in a garment . . ./I do not know its name.*[6]

Many Native American creation stories have surprisingly similar themes to that of Lao-tzu and to our modern cosmology. One of my favorite legends involves an original being called Maheo whose mood, it was said, could determine the state of the universe:

> *At first there was nothing. In the beginning there was noth-ing in all of time and space. Only was there darkness and Maheo. If Maheo was silent, then the Universe was silent. If*

*Maheo was still, then the Universe was still. . . . All around
Maheo was nothingness and silence, age upon age.*[7]

Then Maheo slowly begins to realize the great power he has, the
power to actually create. From that insight, he reasons that "power
is nothing until it has been used to do something." Thus armed with
both power and insight, Maheo concluded it was time for action:

*He took all of time, past and present and future, and gath-
ered it in one hand. Into his other hand he gathered all space.
With these in each hand he clapped. A great clap it was, greater
than thunder. For this clap was the first sound ever heard
in the Universe.*[8]

From that first clap "came all things, and everything from which
all things could be made. . . ."

*Stars came flying out of his hands like sparks from crackling
wood in a fire. Everywhere did the stars fly out and continue
to fly out and burn today everywhere across the night-time
sky. This is how time began and all things began to be made.*

The Big Bang

To a modern astronomer, Maheo's clap of creation is amazingly
similar to the Big Bang theory of the beginnings of the universe[9]
(with the addition of some familiar audiovisual effects like "sparks
from crackling wood in a fire"). Consider too the Old Testament's
creation story of Genesis 1:3. The biblical description brings to light
an important detail, conforming nicely to recent scientific theory. Recall
that on the first day of creation (before Earth had form), God said:
"Let there be light: and there was light."

Physicist Chet Raymo, author of numerous books on astronomy,
believes that the Big Bang was actually misnamed. Instead of Big Bang,
he suggests Big Flash, an event of roughly fifteen billion years ago,
consisting of "an infinitely dense and infinitely hot seed of energy"[10]

coming essentially out of nothingness.[11] And as the universe fed upon its elementary diet of light and gravity waves, the primeval cosmos literally flowed from physical matter into light and back again into matter. At that stupendous, creative moment, cosmologist Gary Bennett writes:

> *Packets of energy called photons raced through the early universe. . . . In a sense the universe at this state was light. . . . Although the temperature had cooled a lot since the inception of the universe less than a millionth of a second before, it was still enormously hot—hundreds of times hotter than a detonating hydrogen bomb. At these temperatures, matter emerged as elementary particles when photon collided with photon. Einstein's famous equation $E = mc^2$ beautifully documents this early era when energy and matter flowed back and forth interchangeably.*[12]

And what happened after this grand opening event of our universe? Professor Raymo states rather simply (I detect here almost a yawn, as if the really hard part was over): ". . . the universe was off and running."[13] Roughly three to four minutes into the Big Bang, astronomers mark the second chapter of creation. The universe had "cooled down" to approximately a billion degrees; its elemental composition consisted of approximately 75 percent hydrogen, 25 percent helium. Virtually all the other elements—elements that go into the making of butterflies and pine trees and water droplets in rainbows, the heavier elements such as carbon and oxygen (among others)—would thereafter be manufactured in the process of star births and star deaths, in the interiors of stupendous fireballs and planetary nebulae (such as Lyra's Ring Nebula) and within the titanic explosions of supernovas, intense zones of radical destructions and fused creations, of atoms compressed into heavier and heavier elements. Hydrogen became helium and then carbon, oxygen, silicon, and iron, ever recycling, ever evolving.

So where do we look? In what direction of the night sky did this stupendous Big Bang event take place? In actuality, we are of the Big

Bang and are currently co-evolving with it after some fifteen billion years. In response to the question "where did it take place?", we learn that the Big Bang "occurred everywhere . . . space itself came into existence with the Big Bang."[14] Indeed, the remnants of the original explosion can still be heard today via microwave radiation that hums smoothly and evenly from each and every part of sky. Unable to pinpoint a single direction, I confess to some disappointment, as if I had run into an invisible barrier in investigating a crucial detail in the broad sweep of my family history.

However the next stage of cosmic evolution does offer greater possibilities for gaining a feeling for, and connection to, our early universe. Bennett continues his description of the beginning moments:

> *As hydrogen and helium spewed forth from the primeval fireball, instabilities in the material formed and grew. Vast clouds of hydrogen and helium, each billions of times more massive than the Sun, fell together under the pull of gravity to make protogalaxies. Inside the newborn galaxies, turbulent regions of gas coalesced under gravity into stars.*[15]

Quasars

We can detect, even "see," these very young, massive galaxies, and within their cores or centers we find highly energized radiation sources astronomers call "quasars." Quasars appear to be fantastic powerhouses, stupendous beacons of radiation dating back to just two or three billion years after the Big Bang. This makes the telescopes that detect them equivalent to scientific time machines, witnessing the universe as it existed four-fifths of the way back to its explosive birth. Though quasar beginnings are still somewhat mysterious, there are some interesting theories about their origins.

Some astronomers suggest that quasars were formed as ancient galaxies collided (not an unexpected event, as the universe was more tightly bound up at the time).[16] Furthermore, it's believed that each of these "quasi-stellar" objects contains one or many black holes, large gravity whirlpools that tug on and pull in matter, distort space itself and thereby capture even light waves that pass nearby. Yet just before the final descent of matter and light into the blackness-of-no-return, some ultrahot elements (heated by friction) beam out powerful waves of radiation like a final cry before the doomed mass disappears into the swirling vortex.

But how could quasars, which are orderly and defined assemblages of matter, have formed so early when other theories suggest that the universe should have been "smooth," its matter spread out evenly? Although researchers have detected faint "ripples"[17] in this background radiation, they continue to disagree as to how quickly and exactly under what conditions these very early galaxies and quasars were formed.

But there is little argument over what you and I can see when we step out on a clear, moonless night. Nearby, in time and space, we have beautiful stars easily accessible with binoculars or simply a bend of the neck, the river of light we call the Milky Way.

Home Galaxy

In his book *Armchair Astronomy*, British author Patrick Moore explains that it would be possible for clusters of stars to escape from a galaxy such as the Milky Way, and he adds, if a cluster could escape, so too might a single star:

> *Once beyond the galactic halo, a star would be beyond the limit of detection . . . particularly if it were a star no more luminous than the Sun. We can visualize the sky as seen from a planet moving round such a star. The night sky would be virtually blank; nothing would be seen apart from dim glows in the extreme distance. It would seem decidedly lonely, and I think we must be grateful that our Sun is not a solitary wanderer in the space between the galaxies.*[18]

As you know, we *do* have an intimate galactic neighborhood, the Milky Way, visible as a lovely, creamy-white trail of countless specks of light seen overhead on a moonless night. In this galactic congregation, there are some 200 billion stars besides the sun! Not only can we easily see our home galaxy, but we also know something about its size and spin. In fact we live in an age when astronomers can accurately pinpoint our earthbound position within the galaxy's vast, wheel-like superstructure.

To bring the Milky Way (symbolically at least) into close proximity, you might begin with a cup of hot water and a spoonful of instant coffee. As you submerge the crystals, give the liquid a clockwise spin. Within seconds, you've created a miniature galaxy out of fine bubbles. A coffee galaxy will usually consist of a central core of densely packed bubbles and well-defined spiral arms that swirl about against a backdrop of inky blackness.

Assuming you make one of these tiny galaxies, and assuming that yours has three or four spiral arms, you have created a surprisingly good representation of the Milky Way. Miniature coffee galaxies are perhaps two or three inches across. The Milky Way, in contrast, is some one-hundred thousand light-years from edge to edge. (Recall that a light year is the distance that light can travel in a year's time, approximately six trillion miles.) In comparison, the closest galaxy that's similar in size to our Milky Way—the great galaxy of Andromeda—is some two million light-years away. Thus, if we could devise a space ship that could move at the speed of light, it would take roughly two million years to make a one-way trip to Andromeda, but "only" a hundred-thousand years to span the Milky Way from edge to edge.

Let's now make another coffee galaxy and this time sketch its unique configuration. So exactly *where* do we reside in respect to the galaxy's central region and flowing arms?

Galactic Orientation

Telescopic data indicate that the Sun's location is neither in the center nor on the very edge of the Milky Way. Our galactic arm, the Orion arm, is between the inner Sagittarius arm and the outer Perseus arm. Actually, we live very close to the inner part of the Orion arm, with our solar system being some 28,000 light-years from the galactic center. Another way of looking at the Sun's "suburban" location is to

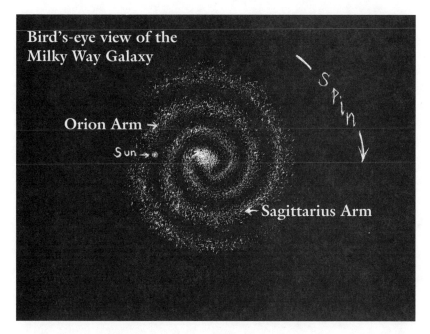

Bird's-eye view of the
Milky Way Galaxy

Spin

Orion Arm →

Sun →

← Sagittarius Arm

think of our position as roughly three-fifths of the way from the galaxy's nucleus to its outer edge.

Perhaps on some cold winter evening, you will find yourself taken in by the Milky Way's great river of stars coursing across the sky. If so, try to find the Charioteer constellation of Auriga (near the famous Pleiades constellation). When you look at Auriga, your line of sight will be roughly into the thick middle region of the Orion arm (in a direction opposite of the galactic center). If, however, you glance toward the bright star Sirius (the Dog Star), your galactic view will be generally toward the outer part of the Orion arm (looking through the outer part of the "tail").

In late summer, you have another opportunity to orient yourself, only then your line of sight will be directed into the interior zones of the Milky Way galaxy. For example, when you look at the constellation Cygnus, the Swan (easily seen in August or September), you'll be looking toward the inner part of the Orion arm, in the direction of the stellar "roadway" that would lead round and round to the Milky Way's central core. Our solar system is, in fact, moving in Cygnus's direction as we circle the galaxy's nucleus.

Now look toward the constellation Sagittarius (the Archer), which is perhaps best seen from a lawn chair on a clear, moonless night in August. (From overhead, North American observers can follow the Milky Way's starry "river" down to the southern horizon.) As you skim the horizon, you may not see a well-defined archer, but something more resembling a teapot.

Now if you would happen to shoot a cosmic arrow toward the spout of the teapot, your arrow would travel through trillions of miles of space—through dark obscuring dust clouds, through massive star clusters, and finally (some 28,000 light-years away) to the very center of the Milky Way's nucleus—into the mysterious heart of our galaxy. Because of the intervening dust, the Milky Way's central core is all but invisible, even to the most powerful optical telescopes, yet it can be "seen" with telescopic instruments that are capable of measuring infrared, X-ray, ultraviolet, and other forms of energy. We also know that the nucleus of the Milky Way is relatively small in size but ultrapowerful in radiation emissions.

On a journey to the Milky Way's center—moving through galactic arms, oceans of star-clouds, and at times, obscuring dark matter—we would come upon:

> . . . *a monstrous pulsing heart for the Galaxy, a core of violence that recapitulates the violence of the Creation itself. The nucleus of the Milky Way Galaxy is apparently the site for cosmic convulsions on the grand scale, perhaps a place where countless suns are swallowed up by a massive gravitational black hole.*[19]

For the backyard viewer facing Sagittarius, there are many other beautiful sights for those who own a pair of binoculars or a small telescope. They include bright clusters, star clouds, and two of the late summer night sky's most stunning nebulae—the Lagoon and Trifid, both located in the neighboring Sagittarius arm of the galaxy.[20]

Hopefully, we can now begin to feel a sense of place within our Milky Way galaxy. Of greatest importance is that we reside at a relatively safe distance, in the "suburbs," away from the lethal pulses of radiation of the central core. But wouldn't it be exciting if there were some way to get a photograph, or perhaps construct a realistic image of what our Milky Way might look like from a distance; to somehow capture its elegant form and inherent beauty in its entirety? Given the hundred-thousand light-year span of our galaxy, humans may never see our home galaxy from such a distant vantage point.

Yet, it is relatively easy to take a peek at a close neighbor—the galaxy of Andromeda—a spiral galaxy surprisingly similar to our own in size and shape.

Locating Andromeda

To find Andromeda's fuzzy congregation of stars, once again it is helpful to have a star chart on hand and, for quick identification, one should use a pair of binoculars.[21] A good time to locate Andromeda is on a moonless night in mid- to late September, when mosquitoes have disappeared and darkness arrives relatively early in the evening. First, can you find the famous North Star via the Big Dipper?

Next, locate the constellation Cassiopeia (the Queen). Her most conspicuous feature in September is a compact group of stars in the shape of a *W* lying on its side (located to the right, or east, of the North Star). If you look closely, you will see that the *W* configuration has two "pointers," both directing your line of sight even further to the east. Now using the upper pointer, sweep your binoculars to the right (roughly the equivalent distance of the Big Dipper's handle), until you come upon a faint, fuzzy smudge.

As you look through your binoculars, Andromeda probably won't be a very spectacular sight. However one can magnify Andromeda not just through the eyes, but also in the mind. Consider Andromeda's 300 billion stars. (How many planets might it have?) And what varieties of life and other amazing creations and fascinations? Consider too that its light has traveled approximately two million years before reaching our eyes. The light from our Milky Way, indeed the light from our Sun of two million years ago (from the era of some of the earliest humanlike creatures such as *Homo habilis*) is now reaching

Andromeda and is perhaps being detected by creatures observing our own Milky Way's soft galactic glow.

Enjoy Andromeda! Consider her swirl[22] and inner secrets. Just pretend for a moment that you are looking at our own galaxy from deep in space. Imagine the billions of suns within this single galaxy and then step back to consider the billions of galaxies and clusters of galaxies that are—at this very moment—unfolding to the hum of creation and the ever-evolving harmony of the Big Bang.

Now return again to the Milky Way, and return to our solar system. Can you make out that lovely blue and white cloud-swirled world below? Haven't you ever wondered what it would feel like to see Earth from such a vantage point in space, to be some lucky observer from high above our planetary neighborhood? Perhaps Louise Young (in her book *The Blue Planet*) said it as well as any:

> *In the photographs of the earth from space, the planet looks like a little thing that I might hold in the hollow of my hand. I can imagine it would feel warm to the touch, vibrant and sensitive. . . . Beneath the mobile membrane of cloud and air are a storehouse of splendors and a wealth of detail. There are rainbows caught in waterfalls, and frost flowers etched in windowpanes, and drops of dew scattered like jewels on meadow grass, and honeycreepers singing in the jacaranda tree.*[23]

And now finally, return down, down to solid earth, to this moment, and to the comfort of knowing "I am home."

CHAPTER 12

Of Time and Place

The animals of the Burgess Shale are holy objects—in the unconventional sense that this word conveys in some cultures. . . .We climb mountains and dynamite hillsides to find them. We quarry them, split them carve them, draw them, and dissect them, struggling to wrest their secrets. . . .They are grubby little creatures of a sea floor 530 million years old, but we greet them with awe because they are the Old Ones, and they are trying to tell us something.

—STEPHEN JAY GOULD

Hold on to the Tao of old in order to master the things of the present.
From this one may know the primeval beginning (of the universe).
This is called the bond of Tao.

—LAO-TZU

Consider once more that tiny coffee-cup galaxy, swirling in miniature, as one might observe it from above the breakfast table. As astronomers now know, our Milky Way has a similar configuration and a similar spinning motion. And within our galaxy, the Sun is carried along with the general flow. Like a parent moving along in a crowd, it pulls its planetary children round and round, slowly circling the Milky Way's dense, star-packed core. In fact, one complete rotation of this great galactic wheel takes approximately 230 million years—a relatively nice and convenient cosmic time unit.

The galaxy would be easier to understand if we could find a way to compress its untouchable enormity into something more tangible. This time, we'll be looking for a model more on a neighborhood scale, to try to experience the galaxy's grandiose rotation while exploring the mysteries of deep time. It might help, for example, to visualize a landmark. Years ago, when I examined an area map, I was surprised to discover that a water tower was precisely one mile from where I was writing (Colfax, Wisconsin). Can we, for a moment, make believe that this water tower is the center of the galaxy, and we will be the Sun, making our 230-million-year circuits round and round? Since this structure will be the nucleus of our cosmic journey, let me take a minute to help you visualize it (undoubtedly you've seen similar water towers in small towns throughout the country).

Our original water tower was built during the First World War. From its four concrete foot pads to its iron weather vane, our tower, at 130 feet, was taller than anything in the surrounding area. Before it was dismantled in 1997 to make way for a larger water tower, it featured a sturdy, steel-plate riveted design. With periodic paintings, the tower probably would have lasted another half century or more to feed pure, well-pumped water to resident households. That it was not harmed during Colfax's devastating tornado of 1958, which destroyed about a third of the village, had always given a feeling of stability and historical continuity to the downtown area.[1]

From a distance, the tower's height and metallic legginess reminded me of a Martian's lethal ray-gun machine from H.G. Wells's *War of the Worlds*. Up close, however, the tower appeared (to my eyes at least) to look more like a tall, friendly, stick character with a funnel hat—resembling the kindly tin woodsman of *The Wizard of Oz*.

Now if we tried walking a large circle around the tower, we would pass through hay fields and neighboring woods, through marshlands and cornfields (and swim twice across the local Red Cedar

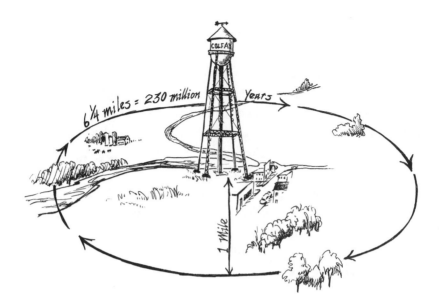

River). With a one-mile radius, the circular distance around the tower would be approximately six miles.

A Trip Back in Time

Keeping Colfax's old water tower in mind, let's assume that with each step, we will be going further and further back in time and each water-tower circuit, like a single rotation of the Milky Way, will represent 230 million years into the past. Let's work out the approximate distance we would have to walk to get back to the Big Bang. (Remember: Each six-mile rotation is equivalent to 230 million years.)

Assuming that the Big Bang occurred fifteen billion years ago (estimates actually vary from twelve to eighteen billion years ago), we would have to make approximately *sixty-five* trips around the tower, or a total distance of about 400 miles. In contrast, to get back to the birth of our planet (about 4.6 billion years ago), we would have to walk around "only" twenty times.

The intense bombardment of our planet by comets and asteroids ended an estimated four billion years ago—or about seventeen water-tower (galactic) rotations. (To see what Earth would have been like after this period, take a look at the Moon with a pair of binoculars. Our cratered satellite offers us a "museum" view of what the planet would be like if unaltered by the movement of continents, the washing of rains, the erosion of winds, and the softening of plants and soils.)

What about Earth's earliest living creatures? One of biology's great surprises is how *quickly* one-celled, self-replicating organisms "came to life" within the primordial waters. Fossils of primitive creatures have been found in rocks that date back 3.5 to 3.8 billion years (only a billion years or so after Earth itself was formed).[2] To walk back to these earliest living microorganisms, we would have to complete some fifteen trips around the tower.

What of the more complex, multicelled creatures such as trilobites and brachiopods? These ancient animals are actually quite recent compared to the very earliest organisms. To see living trilobites and other Cambrian creatures, we need only step back in time about a half billion years (or the equivalent of a little more than two watertower rotations). Consider again the fifteen rotations to the earliest life versus the trilobite's two or two and a half rotations.

For more than four-fifths of biological history, our "ancestors" were represented by relatively simple, one-celled microscopic creatures. It appears that in the journey toward complexity, evolution "rested" (for some three billion years), taking a nap and then suddenly, 530 to 520 million years ago, waking with a start. In an imaginative mood, she began fashioning complex life-forms in a frenzy of creativity. Translating tower rotations into total miles, to go back to the "Cambrian Explosion" of complex life,[3] we would have to walk only fifteen to twenty miles. In contrast, going back to the very earliest life, our trip would be 100 miles or more. (Whew!)

Human Histories

A person might naturally wonder, "Just where do I fit into this evolutionary scheme of things?" I knew I shouldn't have to walk very far to go back to my own particular birth year of 1943. Still I was curious to calculate the representative distance. When I actually entered the appropriate numbers into a calculator, I discovered that *walk* was a rather poor choice of words to measure an individual life span. If a single rotation of 6¼ miles represented 230 million years, this would work out to 6,936 years per foot or 578 years per inch. To "travel" the distance representing my own life would involve an imperceptible movement—a mere ¹⁄₁₆ of an inch—about the width of a toenail clipping!

The oldest person I know was born ninety-five years ago. Her life spans much of our country's history, yet her life's representative distance around the water tower is but an eighth of an inch of a single six-mile galactic circuit. Little wonder that poets and philosophers admonish us to appreciate our minuscule lifetimes: "Teach us to number our days," wrote the psalmist, "so we may apply our hearts unto wisdom."[4] Indeed, who hasn't, at one time or another, reflected upon the evanescent nature of his or her life? Modulating from galactic math to visual metaphor, the Old Testament explains the human situation with unforgettable imagery:

> *As for man, his days are as grass:*
> *as a flower of the field, so he flourisheth.*
> *For the wind passeth over it, and it is gone;*
> *and the place thereof shall know it no more.*[5]

Settled human communities, supported by domesticated grains and livestock, arrived on the scene some 10,000 years ago. How far a walk? A mere seventeen inches. (Not even one full step!) Modern humans (*Homo sapiens*) go back perhaps a quarter of a million years ago—a relatively quick forty-foot walk. Not only is a human life span ultra-brief, but the human entry upon the evolutionary scene is also astonishingly recent.

Gifts from the Glacier

Let's now take a moment to calculate the relative distances to various significant human markers along our trail. Consider, for example, the beginnings of human culture. It has been suggested that an early level of cultural awareness may be inferred from Ice Age cave art as well as from discoveries made from ancient burial sites. We know that Neanderthal peoples buried their relatives with "grave goods" and, in some cases, left flowers at the gravesite (perhaps as a token of affection to the deceased). In one 60,000-year-old site, the famous Shanidar Cave, located in the Zagros Mountains of Iraq, a forty-year-old man was, according to pollen analysis, buried with a bouquet of flowers that included grape hyacinth, St. Barnaby's thistle, bachelor's button, yarrow, and hollyhock. From these finds, one observer suggests evidence of a human community that had components of caring and an elevated level of human awareness:

> . . . *the fact that some kind of ritual had occurred at all in Neanderthal times is eloquent testimony to their heightened awareness of life and death—and of something transcending in life itself. This, surely, is an essence with which we can identify and say: That's human. So far, nothing like it has been seen earlier in the prehistoric record; some kind of threshold appears to have been crossed.*[6]

Of the six miles around the water tower, the Zagros cave site is less than nine feet down our path—about three steps.

Although ritual burials are intriguing, my own personal choice for dating the birth of culture would include the following: humans looking up and trying to make sense of the night sky and the time when humans first learned to make music.

According to archeologist Alexander Marshack, one piece of evidence for early astronomy is an inscribed 30,000-year-old reindeer bone discovered near Les Eyzies, France.[7] Marshack suggests that this artifact may have functioned as an astronomical "notebook," its sixty-nine finely carved marks perhaps representing a period of some 2½ lunar months. We would have to walk a mere fifty-two inches to greet this early hunter/gatherer/astronomer.

And music? Housed in France's Musée des Antiquités Nationales is a 25,000-year-old bird-bone flute crafted by an Ice Age member of the prehistoric Cro-Magnon people.[8]

Visualize, if you will, an early relative of ours— a woman or man (or a boy or girl imitating bird songs?)—who made music on this fragile, four-inch instrument! Within our galactic circuit, this tiny flute is only forty-three inches away, not even the distance—from fingertip to fingertip—of one's outstretched arms.

Some have suggested that hunting technologies might be the best marker for our early cultural and technological development. We do know that flint-tipped spears were made at least 50,000 years ago, and all-wood spears were used a hundred thousand years ago or more.[9] The bow and arrow, according to archaeological research, was invented much more recently, perhaps 12,000 years ago.

These are but a few of the arts and technologies that arose at the edge of the glacier. To the people of the tundra, the ice seemed to say: "Create or perish." One "gift" of the glaciers may therefore have been relatively harsh living conditions that forced our ancestors to be more creative, selecting for sociability, cleverness, and culture as it fashioned among other things, the spear thrower, the astronomer, the artist, and the musician within us. But that time is only a step—or at the most, two steps—from our contemporary point of departure.

Personally, I feel the urge to cover some distance, to witness, some of the older events and environments that shaped our early human relatives. Step with me now past the Great Ice and let us move on to the African tropical savanna some 300 to 600 feet down the path, representing a period of two to four million years ago.

Gifts from the Grassland

A tropical savanna is a relatively dry landscape of perennial grasses and flowers combined with sparse trees (or groves of trees) spread intermittently as far as the eye can see. You have undoubtedly seen savanna scenery as a backdrop to many wildlife documentaries. Picture a mother lion dozing in the shade of an acacia or baobab tree while her cubs roughhouse about, or picture a cheetah accelerating through the grass, chasing a young gazelle as zebras and wildebeests look on.

Some time during the Miocene epoch (five to twenty-three million years ago) a radical climatic change began to bring major cooling and drying cycles and savanna conditions to widespread portions of Africa. Though imperceptible on a human timescale, by 2.5 million years ago,[10] the cooler, dryer climate had profoundly altered the dominant older tropical forests, creating more and more open woodlands and grasslands, the typical African savanna that we see today.

Savanna Economics

For many forest-adapted animals, sources of food became more dispersed. Accordingly, there must have been a survival premium on relative speed and energy-efficient mobility in getting around this new and, in many ways, more difficult grassland habitat. Animals such as camels, horses, and elephants evolved longer legs during this period. For our own ancestors, one very promising way to improve our agility on wide-open grasslands (an improvement over knuckle walking, the typical locomotion method of chimps and gorillas) would be walking on two legs, or *bipedalism.*

Bipedalism is advantageous in another way too: Its inherent vertical posture minimizes solar exposure—a definite plus on the hot and generally dry savanna, where coping with thermal stress would likely be a key factor in survival. Research indicates that when all other aspects of body shape are equal, a quadruped would *gain* some 60 percent more solar heat than would the same animal standing or moving about on two legs![11]

When we consider critical savanna survival economics, the newly evolved upright stance and mode of walking would give our early biped ancestors a definite edge in adapting to a relatively dry landscape. To illustrate, if the more heat-prone quadruped ape required five pints of water per day, its more efficient biped primate relative could get by on something closer to three pints per day.[12]

One gift from the grasslands was therefore a new posture and a unique (indeed revolutionary) way for early proto-humans to move about the savanna. Evidence for early upright posture and bipedalism comes from footprints that are faithfully preserved in the ash of a volcanic eruption of 3.6 million years ago, and also the 3.2-million-year-old "Lucy" skeleton discovered in northern Ethiopia.[13]

Yet, it would take an additional two million years or so before the advantages of freehandedness would be fully realized; that is, the time when our ancestors would begin to use their hands and fingers to fashion artifacts such as digging sticks and storage containers, to throw things, and to carry their few but valuable possessions over the dusty savanna. There is no direct proof, but some paleoanthropologists suggest that, in our three million years of walking the grasslands, we began to learn food sharing,[14] rudimentary language, and culture. This includes the advantages of living within an organized community, that is, of enjoying the economic and social benefits of pooling information, of cooperation, and of creating "political" alliances between related and unrelated groups of individuals.

The advances in social and technological inventiveness (including the use of fire and the making of stone tools with razor sharp cutting edges from *Homo erectus* 1.6 million to 300,000 years ago) became part of the constellation of favorable changes that began on the grasslands of Africa. Walking around the water-tower pathway, we greet our African relatives of the savanna at some 100 to 300 feet into the single six-mile circuit. (The evidence that suggests that all our human ancestors originally came from Africa should, incidentally, enlarge our understanding of our commonality, while minimizing racist attitudes based upon apparent differences.) As we walk through a field of grasses and sparse trees, one might be curious as to why this savannalike landscape seems so pleasing, indeed so familiar. Have we retained some psychological heirloom from that savanna period?

In our minds and bodies, there should be many subtle reference points from our long 3.5 billion year history. How deep then is the relatively recent savanna experience within our psychological makeup?

In his book *Biophilia*, Harvard biologist E.O. Wilson notes that people often recreate elements of the old savanna habitat within contemporary landscapes: "People work hard," Wilson says, "to create a savannalike environment in such improbable sites as formal gardens, cemeteries, and suburban shopping malls. . . ."

Especially telling in this respect are the lovely gardens of the Japanese Heian period (ninth to twelve century) which, according to Wilson,

> *emphasize the orderly arrangement of trees and shrubs, open space, and streams and ponds. The trees have been continuously bred and pruned to resemble those of the tropical savanna in height and crown shape. The dimensions are so close as to make it seem that some unconscious force has been at work to turn Asiatic pines and other northern species into African acacias.*[15]

Indeed, according to presettlement vegetation maps, my area of Wisconsin is an oak savanna in the upland areas, while the glacial outwash plains were once dry savannas (or sand barrens) with Indian grass, bluestems, and intermittent jack pine groves. In selecting this area to live, perhaps settlers were influenced by an invisible tug, some intuitive familiarity with these gently rolling hills, sparse woodlands, and broad grassy vistas.

Earliest Grasses

Continuing our walk into the past, we now make a stop to appreciate the earliest grasses. These remarkable plants were not only critical for the savanna phase of human development, but would eventually be the vegetation of choice in domesticating cereals such as corn, rice, wheat, and barley.

Without grasses, there would have been limited or no agriculture. Of course, without farming, there would have been little need for calendars, currency, or even elementary mathematics—a prerequisite for the development of the sciences. Our stopping point for the very earliest grasses would be about seven-tenths of a mile, representing some twenty-six million years ago.

Gifts from the Forests

Continuing our walk back in time, we step into dense forest, a period beginning about forty million years ago. Checking our distance, we're exactly one mile down the evolutionary path (or one sixth of a single galactic circuit). Here we might meet one of our anthropoid ancestors, who successfully adapted to daytime living after the dinosaurs' demise. By this time[16] our early primate relatives had already evolved many of the essential qualities of forest dwellers, including dexterous fingers for accurate grasping and forward-positioned eyes for stereoscopic, in-depth viewing. During this period, "every leap was an opportunity for evolution," wrote the late science writer Carl Sagan. First summarizing the primate's unique assets, Sagan concludes his comments with an intriguing question:

> . . . *powerful selective forces were at work to evolve organisms with grace and agility, accurate binocular vision, versatile manipulative abilities, superb eye-hand coordination, and an intuitive grasp of Newtonian gravitation. . . . Are our nighttime dreams of flying and our daytime passion for flight . . . nostalgic reminiscences of those days gone by in branches of the high forest?*[17]

Flowers and Birds

Also along the pathway, milestones of the plant world would capture our attention. For example, at 3 to 3½ miles out, we may see early representatives of the angiosperms, or flowering plants. One early flower resembles the beautiful umbrella magnolia that can still be found in relic areas of the Great Smokies.[18] We've walked back in time roughly 120 million years.

At 140 million years (the late Jurassic), we suddenly encounter an early birdlike creature, *Archaeopteryx*. Somewhat larger than a meadowlark, *Archaeopteryx* is a good example of an evolutionary transitional form. Its fossils show unmistakable evidence of bird feathers in addition to the tail, teeth, and foreclaw features of a reptile. As we pass through the *Archaeopteryx's* habitat of dense forests of the late Jurassic, we might just see one (perhaps running along the ground).[19] The plants of this time were various shades of greens and browns, but otherwise the terrain around us would be nearly colorless (remember we're about twenty million years before the colorful flowering plants).

First Mammals

From a pleasant saunter, we may now begin jogging along the pathway, further and further back in time. At the 5½-mile marker (200 million years ago), we are somewhere near the earliest mammals, nocturnal creatures resembling a mouse or a small burrowing shrew.

The earliest mammals could be described as "lively, energetic beings whose living was made at night," according to zoologist John McLoughlin, living in a world of "tree trunks, roots, fallen branches, holes and dinosaurs."[20] The wonderful mammalian adaptations of the Jurassic period of 208 to 144 million years ago include the evolution of specialized teeth[21] and a high degree of sensitivity to sounds, smells, and touch. Consider too that mammals evolved (and still retain to some degree) an impressive ability to see detail in the darkness of night.[22] For our early mammalian ancestors, these dark, moist, microcosms, the interstices of forest floor and undergrowth must have been a fearful world of wakeful midnights, predators, and fleeting insects; surely survival could not have been easy. As McLoughlin's poignant comment puts it: "Our Mesozoic ancestors were heroes, every one."[23]

Dinosaurs

Much easier to spot are the ubiquitous representatives of the magnificent dinosaur clan. On a geological timescale, one must be somewhat impressed with their long-distance run—from the earliest *Herrerasaurus*[24] of about 230 million years ago (one full galactic circuit!) to the dinosaurs' demise sixty-five million years ago. In one 230-million-year circuit around the tower, we would encounter, in one form or another, a representative of these "monster lizards" for approximately 70 percent of our journey. And although there's disagreement about precise dates, it's interesting to note that at approximately each end of the dinosaur time line, we find sobering punctuating marks in Earth's biological history—two mass extinctions.

Many scientists believe that the decisive factor in the most recent extinction (of sixty-five million years ago) was the impact of an asteroid some six to seven miles in diameter.[25] When the dust settled, it left a crater (or what astronomers sometimes call an astrobleme or "star-wound") of approximately 100 miles in diameter.

Numerous animal and plant extinctions would have occurred in the wake of such an impact, triggered in part by a prolonged chill from the sunlight-obstructing dust in the atmosphere, which would severely diminish vital food supplies. In addition, there may have been a high mortality of certain species from titanic waves, from inevitable wildfires, and from highly acidic rains.

The earlier extinction ("the Great Dying" at the end of the Permian period of 250 million years ago) was by far the worst. At least half of all animal families died off on the shores and continental shelves, and perhaps 95 percent or more of the marine invertebrate species became extinct over a relatively short period of time. Reflecting on the mass extinction of 250 million years ago, Chet Raymo wrote:

> *Seventy-five percent of the amphibians and eighty percent of the reptiles were wiped out. Worst hit were creatures that lived in the sea, especially the invertebrates. Corals, crinoids, blastoids, ammonoids, brachiopods, bryozoans, molluscs, foraminifera, and fishes were devastated. The trilobites, which had suffered several earlier disruptions, were finally pushed into oblivion.*[26]

So what happened? Pick your theory. It may have been cosmic events like asteroids, supernovas, or radical climatic change, or perhaps a reversal of Earth's magnetic polarity. Some scientists feel the evidence points to internal geological events like volcanoes[27] or continental drift. We do know that this was the approximate time period when Earth's major land masses were joining together, stitching shorelines together into the huge supercontinent of Pangaea. As this immense landmass formed, it must have eliminated innumerable habitats and marine niches that had existed along the shorelines and the relatively shallow continental shelves.

Once we walk across this Great Dying zone, stepping even further into the past, it's as if we had stepped into a whole new world full of the now-extinct biological riches of the shallow seas of the late Permian. If we were to wade out into the water, we might just find a live trilobite!

We've now come approximately one galactic circuit or the equivalent distance of 250 million years. Putting it in cosmic terms, the Sun has now made a little more than one complete loop around the Milky Way's hub.

Beyond the First Circuit

Although we have walked roughly one complete six-mile circuit, there are many miles, ancient times, and interesting animal and plant life still to see. Consider that interesting aeronautical wizard the dragonfly. Today's dragonflies are small fry compared to some of the giants of the Carboniferous period of 300 million years ago. During this time, one dragonfly in particular, *Meganeura*, had a wing span of almost thirty inches.[28] Another animal that lives today—with direct relatives going back to this period—is the cockroach. Its clan can be traced back to a geological period of some 345 million years ago.

To encounter the very earliest representative, we would have to travel some ten miles or about 1½ circuits around the tower. Nearby on the trail (at 350 million years) are the earliest amphibians (the labyrinthodonts) and their immediate predecessors, the wonderful lobe-finned fish. These animals were probably our own vertebrate ancestors, first to learn to walk upon the land. Exactly why did these fishlike creatures make the great effort to come out of the water in the first place?

One theory states that they had no choice if they were to survive the periodic droughts of the time. And once land mobility became a necessity, consider the anatomical changes that had to be "on-line" for such animals to make their forays from pond to pond over the dry riverbeds. In the modifications of the fish's fins are the roots of our own amazing appendages and their Devonian beginnings:

> *Instead of sitting out the drought, the fish in question would retreat from it, across dry land if need be, and it was this strategic response to the problems of drought that finally endowed the vertebrates with the means of moving from the water to the land. The strategy evolved in a group known as the lobe-finned fish. The basic equipment they employed was common to all the placoderms' descendants: two pairs of fins, one pair just behind the head and another near the tail. . . . The limbs that have carried the vertebrates through the story of life evolved from the fins of the lobe-finned fishes. The basic structure of shoulder, elbow and wrist, and hip, knee and ankle, was already present in the fish that lived 350 million years ago, although its initial significance lay only in enabling the lobefins to support their own weight and to waddle from pond to pond down the riverbed and between lakes as the drought advanced.*[29]

Continuing down our galactic pathway, we now encounter one of the great highlights of our odyssey, a truly memorable landmark in our biological history.

For those readers who have visited the Smithsonian Natural History Museum in Washington, D.C., you may recall a room on the first floor

with an intentionally sloped entrance. Covering the incline is a carpet imprinted with a wave pattern rippling across it. Walking up the incline is like leaving the ocean in preparation to take one's first steps onto a dry beach. Then, in full view on the back wall is a painted panorama depicting a beach scene in the foreground, with rocky hills and cliffs in the distance.

Years ago when walking up this incline, I found emerging from the "water" to be a little unnerving, even spooky. An interpretive sign said it all: "LAND WITHOUT LIFE" (425 million years ago).

Obviously the Smithsonian curators wanted their visitors to experience what the world might have looked like 425 million years ago, a time just before some of the plants and animals began their evolutionary journey out of the sea. At the 425 million year mark, one would see practically nothing above the shoreline except bare rock and vistas of sand.[30] Nothing flying, walking, or slithering about. No flowers, no trees, no plants.

In our galactic walk, we have not quite completed two circuits around the water tower yet on land, all we would see is a barren, dull-grey landscape depicting a scene of lifelessness and loneliness. So what were those remarkable plants and animals that first began to explore the possibilities of life out of the water?

Land Pioneers

The earliest vascular plant may have been the small *Cooksonia* whose finger-length stem rose up and out of the swampy grounds of an equatorial Britain some 410 million years ago. Other land vegetation of this period probably resembled the common liverworts (small flat plants that can be found today in relatively cool, moist, shady, rock environments), or perhaps early versions of the lichens, the symbiotic partnership between fungi and algae. Although we may never know precisely which animal it was that first lived full time (or part time) out of the water, one possible candidate often cited is the *Eurypterid* (a relative of the sea scorpion), which emerged not long after *Cooksonia*.

Other fossil research indicates flea-sized spiders and centipedes may have been terrestrial dwellers as far back as 414 million years ago.[31] But what was so special about this epoch that allowed animals and plants to come out of the sea?

Perhaps most significant was the continuing buildup of atmospheric oxygen. A critical threshold apparently had been reached from millions and millions of years of oxygen produced from sea plants. This altered atmosphere offered planet Earth something truly new "under the Sun," i.e., the formation of an ozone layer capable of absorbing and neutralizing the sun's potentially lethal, ultraviolet radiation and protecting every organism that would venture forth from (or evolve out of) the water. The creation of this delicate, protective membrane must be considered one of the great events of our planet's history, a true guardian of humans and other terrestrial inhabitants. Before this shield was in place, the bare land was dull and grey and sterile. After its creation, "the Earth began to look familiar; a photograph from space would have shown the same blue-green planet that you and I have come to know and love."[32]

Gifts from the Sea

Stepping even further back, say 515 to 545 million years ago, we now enter the relatively shallow continental shelves, alive with myriad life forms. Actually, for me, it is not difficult to envision a Cambrian landscape, since the deposits of that period are relatively easy to find here in west central Wisconsin.

Just a short distance from where I'm writing is a sandstone outcropping my daughter Leslie calls "Ice Cream Mountain." (Why "ice cream?" Because of the distinct layers and shades of color—mainly butterscotch yellows and vanilla whites.) Geologists date this strata of sandstone from approximately 515 million years ago (or roughly two complete circuits around the water tower). Back then, this was probably a beach zone near the relatively shallow water of a warm, inland sea—not unlike the Gulf of Mexico today.

Beach sand! (No wonder the kids like it so much.) Within its creamy sand layers, one can pick up small, eggshell-like, phosphatic brachiopods, about the size and color of my daughter's baby fingernail. Nearby, other outcroppings reveal different fossils, including small trilobite parts and carrot-shaped fossil impressions called *hyoliths.*

Pikaia: First Chordate?

Assuming for a moment that we had been looking for Cambrian life up in British Columbia, we would be encountering some of the

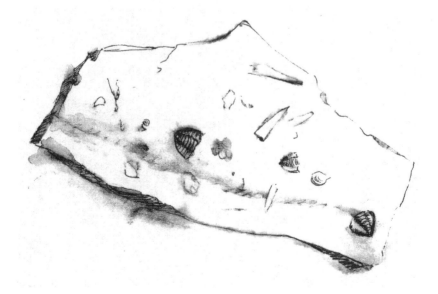

amazing underwater creatures associated with the famous Burgess Shale formation. And if we're lucky, we might just come across an animal who could have been an early ancestor of ours, an ancestor of all vertebrates including all fish, reptiles, and mammals. So who was this Cambrian experiment with a primitive backbone (chordate) design?

Among the earliest chordate designs is the Burgess Shale's *Pikaia gracilens*,[33] a wormlike creature about 1½ inches long who, according to the fossil record, displayed ribboned bands of muscles as well as a notochord (a stiffened rod along the back).[34]

Take a moment, stand up, stretch, touch your spinal column or slide your fingers firmly and smoothly down the furry back of a dog or cat, or admire your pet fish's form, power, and grace, so fully in command of its watery world. When you do, think of tiny *Pikaia*'s contribution to vertebrate design and function, an evolutionary arrow shot out of the Cambrian of some 500 million years ago through fishes and reptiles— a gift from the sea—on through early mammals, primates, and on to you and me.

So how far must we walk the circular pathway to pick up *Pikaia*, or a brachiopod, or one of the trilobites from the Cambrian? It would be about fourteen miles from our starting point or about 2.2 full galactic circuits. (Compare that distance to a mere seventeen inches since the beginnings of agriculture and early civilization.)

But even these half-billion-year-old marine animals are but mere youngsters in life's full history. We need to go back 3.5 billion years to get back to the earliest replicating single-celled life forms. It would be nice if there might be some easy way to make all these exhausting galactic circuits—about fifteen in all. Science writer Loren Eiseley, in his *The Immense Journey*, suggests we can get there (metaphorically) by going down a stairwell:

Reverse the irreversible stream of time. Go down the dark
stairwell out of which the race has ascended. Find yourself
at last on the bottommost steps of time, slipping, sliding and
wallowing by scale and fin down into the muck and ooze out
of which you arose. Pass by grunts and voiceless hissings below
the last tree ferns. Eyeless and earless, float in the primal waters,
sense sunlight you cannot see and stretch absorbing tentacles
toward vague tastes that float in the water. Still, in your form-
less shifting, the you remains: . . . you the entity, the ameboid
being whose substance contains the unfathomable future.[35]

What fun it would be to inspect that distant era, to peek at the great
and grand mystery of life's origins. Is it possible to get back to that
epoch of inert compounds, somehow transforming into living cells?[36]
To get back to that period, we will have to gain some extra velocity—
to spin whole circuits round and round the tower, fifteen full rotations to the earliest life, spiraling back into time, witnessing wonders
that have come and gone. And once we reach the earliest life, we'll
take four more spins back to Earth's coalescing dust and solidifica-
tion. And now why not go all the way back, back sixty-five full rotations to that stupendous flash, the great clap of Maheo and the Big
Bang?

Coming Back

Now reversing ourselves, whirling home through numerous life
zones and witnessing myriad life-forms. For our return trip, Darwin
himself sets the tone:

There is grandeur in this view of life, with its several pow-
ers, having been originally breathed by the Creator into a
few forms or into one; and that, whilst this planet has gone
cycling on according to the fixed law of gravity, from so
simple a beginning endless forms most beautiful and most
wonderful have been, and are being evolved.[37]

Finally, slow down into the final rotation: six miles (the Permian Great Dying), six feet (the beginning of Ice Age culture), six inches (written history begins), and finally the final fraction of an inch, a snip of a toenail (you and me). Now, finally, descending into this minute, this space—momentary home to our own time and place.

CHAPTER 13

The Copycat Species

That the deer does experience sensations, that it carries knowledge of how to orient in the land, of where to find food and how to protect its young, that it knows well how to survive in the forest without the tools upon which we depend, is readily evident to our human senses. That the apple tree has the ability to create apples, or the yarrow plant the power to reduce a child's fever, is also evident. To humankind, these Others are purveyors of secrets, carriers of intelligence that we ourselves often need. . . .

—DAVID ABRAM

Consider once more our last galactic circuit and particularly the final forty-foot segment within the six-mile circumference that represents our species' 250,000-year evolution. What then was it that nature handed to our species, the unique gift of *Homo sapiens* intelligence?

In searching for the answer along the evolutionary pathway, we would no longer be looking for finger-bone fragments, fossil teeth, bipedal footprints (or that lovely, little bird-bone flute). Instead, we would be searching for something invisible, tantalizingly cryptic, one of nature's works in progress.

What exactly is the nature of our intelligence or, for that matter, of intelligence itself? Does anyone know? Is there such a thing as nature's own version of intelligence as a working concept? And does this "intelligence" have a purpose?

In the game of evolution, the natural world seems organized to create myriad forms—specialized "machines," if you will—that bridge generations from egg to egg, seed to seed, thereby preserving unique arrangements of genetic material. It's a creative trade show of organic innovations, where individuals work to survive and reproduce within specific habitats while exploiting resources from various ecological niches. In this context nature would be judged on how effectively its biological processes are able to keep gene pools intact, by creating with care and workmanship, with durability and predictability, organisms capable of successfully completing their life cycles. Also, should the environment change, the behavior or physical traits of the organisms might also evolve to confront the problems and challenges of an altered environment. If the organism is "intelligently" designed (at this micro level), its genes or similar genes will, more often than not, be safely delivered into the next generation.

Primordial Pulse

Yet on a macro level, it's doubtful whether nature is really interested in any given species at all (considering that most species that have evolved are extinct).[1] Nature's ultimate "purpose" may be simply to preserve that primordial pulse bequeathed to the very earliest organisms some three and a half billion years ago and then transmit that rhythm round after round, circuit after circuit, as the great galactic wheel turns about its hub.

Considering both micro and macro objectives, nature has shown an impressive capability in fulfilling the mission of maintaining that primordial rhythm. (In fact, here music may be a better metaphor than building machinery.)

Consider for a moment life's very modest beginnings, which eventually modulated into many beautiful biological compositions (including ourselves) throughout the many geological eras. Like a Beethoven or Bach embarking upon musical variations upon a theme, beginning with a simple melody or tune and soon building into exquisite sounds and forms, nature composes music of unarguable genius!

Minnesota poet and essayist Bill Holm once wrote about the great musicians such as Bach and Beethoven. As I now read his comments, I found a workable analogy linking musical variations to nature's myriad variations of form and beauty:

> *I am interested in the idea of Variation. It is a curious fact that often the most ingenious and intense pieces by the greatest composers, which seem to accumulate a lifetime's whole knowledge and feeling into themselves, are long sets of variations that begin with a trifle, with nothing, and build enormous, sublime, ecstatic, often humorous structures . . . the architect stands back and smiles, inviting you to admire his fantastic powers.*[2]

Holm reminds his readers that Beethoven began his great piano work—the "Diabelli Variations"—with a simple "ta-tum" waltz tune, while Bach opened the famous "Goldberg Variations" with an unadorned dance melody from a child's musical instruction book. Nature, in turn, began its "Variations" with a simple, prokaryotic, replicating cell approximately three and a half billion years ago.

If nature can thus play so whimsically with its notes, combining them with fun and abandon, with successes and mistakes, why can't we too play with various ideas and observations and try to tease out a theory concerning our question about the nature of intelligence?

Variations and Stability

So again, what devices and strategies work to maintain the vast variety of gene pools and nature's primordial pulse? The most basic device, of course, is the cell's genetic code, made malleable via mutation and sexual reproduction. In this context, sex was an innovation "designed" to supply novel genetic combinations that, when favorable, permit successive generations to adapt to new circumstances—a sort of biological "insurance policy" that enhances the chances of generational survival against a changing environment.

On the other hand, numerous animal and plant groups have gone on and on and on with little design change or genetic tinkering at all. These "intelligently" constructed organisms must be must given good grades in satisfying the criteria of survival, reproduction, and gene-pool durability. Among the complex organisms we've already mentioned, recall the trilobite's long run through geologic time. And of biology's living fossils, a good report card would go to various mosses, ferns, liverworts, horsetails, and the ancient ginkgo tree; and among animals, crocodiles, frogs, turtles, horseshoe crabs, dragonflies, cockroaches, sponges, starfish, chambered nautilus, and certain species of worms[3] would undoubtedly receive a high grade. Each of these creatures had ancient relatives that were similar (and in some cases, nearly identical) to species living today. Perhaps the valedictorian of the class would be the *Lingula*, a small brachiopod who *still* lives in intertidal sediments and, for all practical purposes, is unchanged from relatives of 450 million years ago.[4]

Genetic Intelligence

What other ways has nature impressed us with its intelligence? It would perhaps be fun to swap stories of personal observations. As you have probably noted, I sometimes get into a habit of giving grades to my friends of the natural world. I once gave a *D* to a birch that grew out at an angle from a rocky perch. Why the low grade? Because its center of gravity was growing away from its relatively flimsy anchor of support. Sure enough, one day I came by and found that this lovely tree had tumbled down the rocky slope.

In contrast, I once gave an *A* to a grove of box elder trees growing on a steep lake bank. Although the locals deride it as a junk tree and sometimes cut box elders down with few regrets, to me the box elder is impressive because of its uncanny ability to survive in degraded soils and also for preventing erosion, which maintains topsoil for future box elders. Who could not be impressed by these graceful trees stretching out their trunks, like long necks, over the water, into the open commons of bright sunlight? One could almost say that lake-bank box elders, with their amazing ability to seek and find sunlight, have achieved a kind of "mobility."

The more I get to know trees, the more impressed I become with what looks like a kind of rudimentary "intelligence." Though subjective, I'd also give good grades to a white oak I observed one spring. With amazement, I witnessed its odd but effective defense against a severe insect larva attack. The oak's tender, half-grown spring leaves had already been eagerly devoured. Stripped of all foliage, the tree appeared finished. What I observed was really a strategy of patience. The tree sacrificed its first set of leaves to the invaders. (If it could communicate, its message to the insect larvae might have been: "Go ahead, gorge yourselves. Get on with it.")

The invasion came and went, and within a week, the attackers mysteriously disappeared, perhaps to continue their transformations elsewhere. There was a short period of waiting, and then slowly, miraculously, the oak began growing a second set of leaves. Its genetic intelligence seemed to know something about the timing of insect invasions, holding off the secondary leafing, but just how did this kind of intelligence come about?

Natural Selection

Based on Darwin's theory of evolution through natural selection, we can explain the oak's unique response something like this: In an earlier period, undoubtedly some individuals or species had this timing mechanism and others didn't. When insects attacked, those that had the defense mechanism lived. Those that didn't were phased out (since the vulnerable tree would not be able to reproduce). Those that lived implanted the successful response into the genetic instructions of subsequent generations (including the oak I observed).

Using this definition of nature's genetic intelligence, insects too would be at the head of the class. If you watch closely a field sprayed year after year with pesticides, you may witness a kind of evolution taking place through the appearance of so-called "superbugs."

The secret, of course, is in the insects' relatively rapid rate of reproduction. After successive generations, some insects will be born with an immunity to the pesticide. They, in turn, become insect "factories" for offspring who will continue to enjoy the favorable genetic makeup. In a relatively short time, new varieties of immune super-bugs will be back on the plants, munching as the spray truck chugs on by.

Thinkers and Strategists

Now if we define intelligence more conventionally, as the ability to contrive ways (or visualize strategies)[5] to solve problems and ultimately get what one wants or needs from the immediate environment, then chimpanzees should make the honor roll. Chimps have learned (among other things) to fabricate and use tools: Finding and fashioning a stick to extract termites and modifying a leaf to sponge up water from hard-to-reach places are two examples that have been observed in the wild.[6]

From my observations, one animal who nearly always discovers ways to get what it wants is the squirrel. For starters, consider how difficult it is to build a completely squirrelproof bird feeder! By demonstrating flexibility in behavior through trial and error, squirrels seem able to crack all codes designed to keep them out.

Having experienced such frustrations with my bird feeder, I was not surprised to learn that squirrels may have also mastered the art of maple syrup tapping. As the story goes, a zoology researcher once observed a group of red squirrels lapping maple sap that he initially thought had been dripping from random tree wounds. But upon closer inspection, the investigator (Bernd Heinrich) concluded that the squirrels had actually been tapping the trees.

> *The red squirrels were doing more than opportunistically visiting tree wounds where there happened to be sugar. They were methodically making the wounds themselves which served as*

sugar taps . . . the squirrels always moved on almost instantly after making a bite, not waiting for any immediate reward. Taps were revisited only hours or days after they were made. . . . I was surprised that the squirrels were able to distinguish between even the red and sugar maple (a task that is daunting to most college seniors enrolled in a winter ecology class).[7]

In addition, these particular squirrels made a point of ignoring the runs of sap that had a relatively low content of sugar (4 to 5 percent), preferring instead the evaporated sticky glazed streaks where the sugar content often exceeded 55 percent.

Establishing and maintaining a Maine sugarbush should indeed be the basis for an excellent squirrel report card; it's in such observations that these animals appear to be using a mode of intelligence perhaps closer to our own. But in one personal encounter, I was convinced that a representative of this genus who lives in and about the Grand Canyon was, I'm embarrassed to say, smarter than myself.

Those readers who have visited the Grand Canyon may recall the signs that remind visitors, "DO NOT FEED THE WILD ANIMALS." On a recent trip, I, too, dutifully read the park rules and was in full agreement with its message. I even made a mental note that under no circumstances would I give in to any beggar—big, little, friend, or foe.

About an hour into my morning descent along the Bright Angel Trail, I decided to stop and have breakfast. A little rock squirrel appeared from under a slab of sandstone, obviously intending to join me in my solitary picnic. But I explained as best I could: "Sorry, the park rangers don't want me to feed you, so you're really wasting your time."

Moments later I repeated: "You're not getting anything from me, do you hear?" But he was determined, demonstrating an annoying degree of persistence as he crept closer and closer. Still, I was able to finish my breakfast, and (I am proud to say) I wasn't about to give in. "Sorry little friend," I remarked as I zipped up my backpack. Soon I was all ready to get up, dust myself off, and get back on the trail. The squirrel had now moved closer, perhaps two or three feet away;

he was, in fact, preparing to pull out strategy number two from his bag of tricks: sitting up like a begging dog. Yet I was still resolved not to give him anything (though I confess that I was somewhat entertained).

"Very cute," I said.

And then it happened. This sad-looking fellow made another attempt, he had one more trick up his sleeve that, to this day, leaves me embarrassed and humbled. While sitting up, he suddenly appeared to get skinnier and skinnier. Though I am not absolutely sure, I think I saw his rib cage. (Was he sucking in his stomach?) Anyway, something deep inside me stirred. "Boy is this guy hungry," I thought. "It certainly wouldn't hurt to give him a corner of my cheese sandwich."

So I unzipped my backpack, rummaged about, pulled out a sandwich, and as I was breaking off a corner, he suddenly lunged at my hand. Startled, I dropped everything. He snatched the sandwich and, with remarkable speed and energy, dragged it over a large flat rock, and then disappeared from view. I ran around the rock, stooped down and, as my eyes adjusted to the dim light, I could just barely make him out in his dark, safe cavern. He sat there calmly, quietly munching on my lunch.

Considering what happened, considering the squirrel's apparent "knowledge" of psychology and his patience and persistence, just who had demonstrated superior intelligence?

In measuring my own ability to learn, I now have at least one criterion: not to repeat my mistakes. The next time I walk down into the Grand Canyon, I will certainly be on my guard for crafty squirrels. (Though I'm worried that in that little rodent brain, there may be even more subtle ways of extracting my bread and cheese.)

Continuing this line of thought, one new and interesting criterion for human intelligence could be just what one could learn from this squirrel. In other words, what in his maestro performance could I have extracted from him to help me and my descendants survive?

Mentors and Mythology

My guess would be that if our early ancestors had encountered such a squirrel, the animal might have earned the status of mentor or teacher.[8] Our ancestors might have remembered this little creature, both in story and myth, for his boldness and craftiness. If he taught some important lesson (such as persistence and the need to proceed by trial and error) and that lesson had helped our people survive various adversities, we might have honored him in different ways. Perhaps, for example, we would call ourselves the Squirrel Clan.

Furthermore, if our family had lived in the Grand Canyon area, where art in the form of petroglyphs and pictographs was common, a future archaeologist might see a depiction of a squirrel, or perhaps there would be a petroglyph of a squirrelman, a creature with the head of a squirrel and the body of a man. A creation story might then be told and retold relating the idea that the first people were much like the squirrels: "They displayed patience, diligence, and despite numerous setbacks, considerable wisdom . . ." Would it be farfetched to say that our tribe or group might someday collect such stories and myths into a "holy book," from which we could read something like the following:

> *But ask the beasts, and they will teach you;*
> *the birds of the air, and they will tell you;*
> *or the plants of the earth, and they will teach you.*[9]

Nature's Copycat Species

Have we, all along, been asking the beasts and plants to teach us? Was one important element of our evolution learning how to observe nature's vast array of intelligences and then imitating their proven ways and means? Have our own mental and cultural powers, over time, been nudged along by animal analogies and mythological metaphors learned through humbly watching, listening to, and imitating nature's mentors? Have they been shaped by experimenting (monkeying around) then inviting the connective simile or image—"crafty like a coyote," "wise as the bear (or owl)"?

Somewhere in the mystery of that forty feet of human evolution, we became (I believe) nature's copycat species, a creature persistent in curiosity, with a brain wired to make analogies between the natural world and our own struggle on the African savanna and beyond. Add uprightness, free hands, fine-tuned manipulative fingers, and you will encounter an animal that carefully observes its natural world and will not hesitate to plagiarize the myriad manifestations of nature's "intelligence." Need more examples? Consider the intriguing theory that the stone arrowhead may have been first conceived in relation to the beak of a bird:

It is not improbable, and would be in full accord with early man's mentality, that the arrow represents a materialized metaphor. When the hunter saw the animal fleeing unattainably beyond his reach, he would have thought that a bird with its wings could easily catch it. Since he was not a bird and also had none at hand . . . he finally attached a beak to one end of a small stick and feathers to the other end. In other words, he created the artificial bird, the arrow, which flies swift as lightning through space and pierces the flank of the fleeing deer.[10]

Think of the many survival lessons we could have learned from close attentiveness and good behavior in nature's classroom! In the article on maple syrup and red squirrels, Dr. Heinrich asks: "How did humans learn that a nearly tasteless, watery liquid found in maple trees can be made into a delicious food?" He suggests that the squirrels themselves may well have been the Native American's maple syrup teachers.[11]

Similarly, it's been suggested that the Chinese "invented" paper by the careful observation of wasps building paper nests.[12] Did humans adopt adobe from the mud-dauber wasps? Did we learn the art of weaving from the African weaver birds?

I was intrigued to learn that hatha yoga, the stretching exercises from India, came to light from the careful observation of animals and plants. "It's the natural thing to do," a yoga instructor noted, adding that her "posture work is taken from observation of life—how animals move, how young children, even trees move."[13] It has been said that if the knowledge of hatha yoga were ever lost, it could be rediscovered through careful observation of the animal kingdom.[14] The Chinese martial art of T'ai Chi is also based in part on the imitation of animals, particularly birds and the weaving motion of snakes.[15]

The Ojibwe tribe of Wisconsin has been known to watch the black bear to locate healthful plants. A tribal member claimed that "the bear pays attention to herbs; it eats roots from the earth, and acorns, berries, and cherries."[16] Reaffirming the "wisdom" of the bear,

Sioux medicine man John Lame Deer describes how some people, in their dreams, may learn of the bear's plant knowledge:

> *The bear is the only animal that one can see in a dream acting like a medicine man, giving herbs to people. It digs up certain healing roots with its claws. . . . Many songs of the bear dreamers end with the words* Mato hemakiye— *a bear told me this. Then everybody knows who gave this medicine man his powers.*[17]

Want to learn how to swim? John Muir's father advised his son to "go to the frogs and they will give you all the lessons you need."[18] This advice, reverberating with Old Testament overtones, proved successful for the future naturalist.

Interestingly, modern medical researchers are taking the advice of "going to the frogs," not to learn how to swim but to investigate chemicals that may save human lives. Michael Zasloff of the National Institute of Child Health and Human Development says that the robust African clawed frog contains a natural antibiotic that may someday be synthetically produced and used for treating children with severe burns.[19] Here is but one illustration of how science and pharmaceutical researchers are carrying out our evolutionary mandate of first observing nature and then replicating her wonders for human health and welfare. It is also a good illustration of why we should make every effort to preserve as many of the world's animal and plant species as possible.

Unfortunately, frogs, toads, and other amphibians are diminishing in numbers throughout the world.[20] Although the reasons for these losses are not completely clear, it is likely that human activities play an important role. Ozone depletion and an increase in UV-B radiation is apparently one reason for their decline.[21] What then might be the practical and ethical implications?

On the ethical side, consider the fact that amphibians have been around for some 250 million years, surviving the Great Dying at the end of the Permian period, even surviving that stupendous cosmic collision at the end of the Cretaceous—the probable death knell of the dinosaurs some sixty-five million years ago. And now, in less than one step along the galactic pathway, a step dominated by a rapid expansion of human populations and technologies, a number of amphibian groups are becoming threatened. Others face the very real possibility of extinction.

On a more utilitarian level, the continuous destruction of diverse habitats for a wide range of plants and animals is nothing less than the mass murder of Earth's living teachers, eliminating forever the many creative and potentially useful wonders of nature's evolutionary workshop.

Metaphoric Understandings

In summary then, perhaps one element of human intelligence involved imitation, and then clothing that imitative knowledge with metaphoric and symbolic understandings that can be quickly transmitted throughout traditional cultures via story, myth, and poetry.

Putting it slightly differently, within our crucial forty feet, human intelligence has, I believe, climbed an incline of metaphors, analogies, similes, and imagery, and in that ascent, we have been able to enjoy a higher and higher perspective of the universe and our place within its grandiose spectacle. Like synapses between brain tissue, the similes and metaphors help us connect and condense as we attempt to make sense of our perplexing world. Consider again the Native American's creation myth, "like sparks from crackling wood in a fire;" and the Old Testament's "as for man, his days are as grass."

Consider too the possible analogies from our bird mentors: In artifact its beak "became" an arrowhead, and in poetry, the possibilities for metaphor might be taken a step or two further. In the following poem, the bird's pain may be used to communicate human loneliness and loss:

Leaving me (no word)
was like—thump against glass—
remember that poor bird?

Something in the human mind searches for an image or hungers for a memorable metaphor, which once found, confers universal satisfaction and wide-spread nods of recognition. Recently, my daughter was watching *Romeo and Juliet*, when I came in to eavesdrop. Poor Juliet was destined to fall in love with her family's "enemy," yet we saw that she gained some comfort, not by dwelling upon the convoluted tangle of Verona's feuding families but by embracing a metaphor. Remember her famous speech:

What's in a name? That which we call a rose/
by any other name would smell as sweet.

Clues to the puzzle of our unique intelligence—our species' metaphoric communication skills—were perhaps with us all the while as we walked the path, clues tucked deep into our minds, from old memories taken from childhood poems, readings, and our parents' stories. (Surprised, I'm now feeling perhaps as Dorothy did in the *Wizard of Oz*. Remember when she was told that she actually had the power to go home? Dorothy needed only to express what she had already known to be true.)

Again walk this precious forty feet with me, construct images, invent metaphors and analogies, feel free to copycat any way you please. Now that I am attuned to noticing them, it's amazing how many illustrations I've come across:

➤ A chess-buff friend of mine told me that he pretends there's a mountain in the middle of the chess board. He also imagines a river flowing by from the queen's side toward enemy territory. These metaphoric images help him gain a strategic position as the game proceeds. His advantage over a computer chess program? The mountain/river analogy.

➤ From a TV documentary detailing the 1962 Cuban Missile Crisis, we learn that the United States and the Soviet Union were days, even hours from nuclear war. Khrushchev, worried that events were moving past the point of no return, sent a lengthy teletype message to President Kennedy on October 26. In this message, Khrushchev crafted the perfect metaphor for the escalating danger: "Mr. President," Khrushchev wrote,

> *We and you ought not to pull on the ends of the rope in which you have tied the knot of war; because the more the two of us pull, the tighter that knot will be tied. And the moment may come when that knot will be tied so tight that even he who tied it will not have the strength to untie it.*[22]

Did such an unadorned but powerful metaphor help save humanity from nuclear annihilation? If so, it would have been a good use for a very old evolutionary pathway of our species—we who, ironically, have the power to destroy civilization by applying a wrong thought to a wrong technology.

> ➤ A third example comes from the writings of Buddhist monk Thich Nhat Hanh. Perhaps we shouldn't be surprised to come across another use of a mountain/water metaphor, but unlike the chessboard illustration above, Nhat Hanh's imagery is intended to help readers deal with emotions through visualization. Compare the following quote with the chess-board analogy described above:

> *We have to practice conscious breathing so that we can learn how to cope when difficult moments come and strong emotions take hold of us. 'Breathing in, I see myself as a mountain. Breathing out, I feel solid. Mountain/Solid. . . .' Near the mountain, there is a lake with clear, still water reflecting the mountain and the sky with pristine clarity.*[23]

> ➤ A few pages later, in an intriguing coincidence, he makes use of precisely the same metaphor Nikita Khrushchev used so effectively in his warning to President Kennedy. Instead of describing a global conflict between nations, here the

knot imagery imaginatively represents the dangers of unresolved inner conflict:

In Buddhist psychology, the word samyojana *refers to . . . fetters, or knots. When someone says something unkind to us, for example, if we do not understand why he said it and we become irritated, a knot will be tied in us. . . . They need our full attention as soon as they form, while they are still loosely tied, so that the work of untying them will be easy. If we do not untie our knots when they form, they will grow tighter and stronger.*

Gift from the Cocklebur Clan

One of my favorite stories on the creative use of imagery, metaphor, and natural analogy involves NASA—an agency with a reputation for using nothing but high-tech, space-age materials. Their particular need in this story, however, was low-tech, even refreshing in its ordinariness.

NASA was looking for a fastening device for space suits, one that could easily be manipulated with bulky gloves. As the story goes, NASA engineers brainstormed the problem through word associations and visualizations. One image simply involved people "running through the forest and having thorns stick to the clothes."[24] They then tried to think of something in the woods that might grip with thousands of thornlike fasteners, something perhaps like a cocklebur with its dozens and dozens of small hooks. What then was their invention?[25] Velcro! Therefore, the next time you use Velcro (perhaps kneeling down to remove a sleepy child's tennis shoe), reflect not upon the genius of humans but the ingeniousness of nature and that curious mode of evolutionary intelligence, the analogy, so innately human. Hold onto your memorable metaphors of myth and story, enjoy your analogies, have them cling to your mind—like cockleburs:

"Juliet's rose"

"like the beak of a bird"

"his days are as grass"

"the knot of war"

"I see myself as a mountain"

Listen carefully to our amazing connective language opening the door to human understanding, going back even to the beginning of creation itself —to Maheo's clap scattering stars like "sparks from a crackling wood!"

Meadowlark and Flowering Spurge

The scene, for me, is now so very familiar: not far ahead is home. To my left (out of sight) I heard the music of a meadowlark. To my right, I can see a plant in bloom—the flowering spurge. And somewhere within this flower's simple beauty, I sense whispers of metaphor and meaning. The spurge—*Euphorbia corollata*—is not a particularly showy or colorful flower, but more an embroidery of daytime stars elevated above the common green. Sometimes its small blossoms are like fireworks—tiny flashes bursting into the air—usually in tight, full clusters. At other times, they rise up in starry circles, recalling (especially in the glow of twilight) the lovely ring nebula of Lyra and of that August night my daughter and I looked up to the heavens.

I wonder if she still remembers our promise to return to those questions about the universe, and to our curious inquiries about human existence—like that night long ago when we talked of meteors and meanings, of futures and feelings, as the constellations Harp, Swan, and little Dolphin crept slowly across a darkening sky?

CHAPTER 14

Music, Metaphor, and Meaning

We are like a musician who faintly hears a melody deep within the mind, but not clearly enough to play it through.
—THOMAS BERRY

. . . everything is gift. The degree to which we are awake to this truth is the measure of our gratefulness. And gratefulness is the measure of our aliveness. . . .
—DAVID STEINDL-RAST

. . . our eyes contemplate with admiration and transmit to the soul the wonderful and varied spectacle of the universe.
—HENRY THOREAU

Who are we? What does it mean to be human? Like the meadowlark and the flowering spurge, do we too have a melodic part within the harmony of nature's beginnings and subsequent variations on a theme? If so, how might we describe our music, our meanings and purposes?

After the many circuits around the tower, we should perhaps feel a little more oriented to both our time and place, but a cosmic journey soon suggests further explorations. Are we more than an interesting branch of mammals or a complex cultural variation of the primates? Are we more than nature's ultrakeen observers, the copycat species? Are there any clues to how our versatile mind fits in, our large-brained abilities, our sciences, technologies, our insatiable drive for discovery and knowledge?

Habitats of Technology

After completing my walk along the pathway, I returned to the house. As I stepped inside, I noted that my own personal life seemed far from the natural world of birds and flowers, far from living under the sun or Milky Way. Instead of living within nature, I dwell in habitats of manmade technology, not of nature's web of life, but in an ecology of machinery, steeped in artificial dependencies and fabricated artifacts of all sizes and shapes: Here's a TV. There's a radio and stove. Overhead, I see a synthetic sun, and over that, a roof sheltering my artificial abode. Instead of wearing fur, I slip on a wool sweater and warm socks.

In the kitchen, I see a coffeemaker and a plastic container full of peanut butter cookies, each seemingly more and more remote from nature. Outside, an aging Ford sits in the drive. (In the natural world, is there anything analogous to the automobile's wheel and axle? I can't think of anything.)

Through the window, I can just barely make out the faint lights of a distant jet hurtling travelers westward. Nearby, electricity and telephone lines loop from pole to pole into the house. Indeed, I am impressed by our advanced technology and our culture, by my eyeglasses and this telescope that extends one's sight. I'm impressed, too, with the shelves of books, the old *Geographics* and our large new dictionary. Despite the benefits of these things, I sometimes feel depressed when I consider how "plugged in" I am.

Harnessed to visible and invisible tools, it's as if I were all wired up—like those large connectors with multicolored wires going every which way, regulating both flow and function. As time passes, our wad of wiring changes; new connections are added, others subtracted.

Computers, Cars, and Big Macs

Today, almost everyone is exposed to direct or ambient effects of computers, gene-splicing, global marketing of armaments, mass-produced toys, Big Macs, the international grids of transport, and the ubiquitous entertainment and information "highways." What do they mean? How will these pervasive artifacts affect you, me, the world? Who really knows?

I doubt if we even know what that well-known artifact the automobile has done or is doing to us. Many years ago I recall watching an "educational" documentary film about the history of the automobile industry. It had as its centerpiece theme the "life and times of Henry Ford," giving considerable praise to Ford's amazing assembly line and wonderful Model T. Toward the end of the film, viewers were brought up to date with film clips from the forties and the affluent decades of the fifties and sixties. As the documentary rolled on, one began to get the feeling that because of the automobile, something wonderful, even beautiful had taken place throughout the land. Consider the documentary's eloquent case for progress:

> *The whole nation has become swift and mobile. Flowing along over a great network of highways, more than three million miles long, and constantly growing, the American Road has lifted itself high over the muddy ruts of fifty years ago. . . . The people of the city have been able to move into quiet communities. Full of sun and fresh air, it seemed like almost living in the country. . . . Today's worker no longer has to live next to the plant that employs him. His home is in pleasant surroundings and he drives to work.*[1]

How well I recall in the film that young (and very pretty) woman—her long blond hair billowing up in the breeze—at the wheel of her new, sleek, red car. She beamed, as if intoxicated by the beauty of the sunset and the power of her car as she delighted in the unquestioned "freedom of the road." (One has to hand it to Ford's Public Relations Department. They do knew how to get the attention of high school boys and girls!) Again, the industry point-of-view is worth quoting:

> *... perhaps the most wonderful thing about the American Road is the freedom it gives us. You only have to get in your car and start driving to feel it. The American Road! What magnificent vistas open up before us. . . . We have come a long way since the quadracycle and the Model T. In fifty short years our whole way of life has changed. We have accomplished much, but the achievement to come will dwarf our own. The American Road stretches ahead of us, always toward a new horizon. We are all traveling along that road. All moving toward an even better tomorrow.*

The movie clickety-clicked through its final scene and film credits, leaving the classroom in momentary darkness.

I have often wondered how many teachers back then had the time or inclination to question the validity of Ford's assumed values and their grandiose vision of the future. At some point it might have been interesting to introduce the students to some of the quirky critics of materialism and industrialization. What would they have thought for example of Ralph Waldo Emerson's, "Things are in the saddle, and ride mankind."[2] (Do we ride in the car, or does it ride us?) Also recall our friend Henry David Thoreau—a home-grown critic of overconsumption and new technologies who once commented so simply yet powerfully, "Men have become the tools of their tools."[3]

The late E.F. Schumacher, author of *Small Is Beautiful*, maintained that our products and technologies should display, at a minimum, the characteristics of beauty, simplicity, and permanence.[4] How would the U.S. automobile industry fare under such a trio of values?

A more recent critic, Jerry Mander, asks some intriguing questions in his book *In the Absence of the Sacred*, questions that might have been interjected at appropriate places in the film. For example, Mander wonders how the public would have felt about cars had they been able to see (early on) some of the eventual side effects:

What if the public had been told that the car would bring with it the modern concrete city? Or that the car would contribute to cancer-causing air pollution, to noise, to solid waste problems, and to the rapid depletion of the world's resources? What if the public had been made aware that a nation of private car owners would require the virtual repaving of the entire landscape, at public cost, so that eventually automobile sounds would be heard even in wilderness areas?[5]

As for the economic assessment of car companies in general, and Ford's assembly line in particular, Mander asks:

What if it had been realized that the private car would only be manufactured by a small number of giant corporations, leading to their acquiring tremendous economic and political power? That these corporations would create a new mode of mass production—the assembly line which in turn would cause worker alienation, injury, drug abuse, and alcoholism? That these corporations might conspire to eliminate other means of popular transportation, including trains?

In respect to the woman driving (alone) or the "happy" worker commuting from his suburban home, Mander wonders:

What if there had been an appreciation of the psychological results of the privatization of travel and the modern experience of isolation?

Similar questions could be asked about the possible consequences or potential side effects of any scientific breakthrough, technology, or mass-consumed product that an industry designs, fabricates, and successfully markets to the masses.

Trio

In earlier stages of our cosmic journey, our animal origins were emphasized. Later, human culture came to the fore as our hunting and gathering ancestors had to adapt and survive the rigors of climate change (such as the Ice Age) and the emergence of new habitats.

Now a new "tonality" should be added, our relatively recent advances in science and the subsequent spin-offs in the form of new technologies and mass consumerism. Indeed, this newer economic/technological component seems out of balance and thus the louder, more discordant theme within our "musical composition." Generally this component is not orchestrated for aesthetics or pure discovery, but for profit. As we noted earlier, the consequences of pervasive products and technologies are often unpredictable and, at times, seem to be out of control, yet like children, we often accept whatever happens to drift by, seduced by enhanced convenience or the propaganda of novelty. Or we simply sit on our couches—pushing buttons—while inviting into our living rooms, indeed into the depths of our minds, whatever titillates our sensibilities or happens to be placed within view.

I confess to some of the weaknesses of my fellow *Homo consumerus* when I lounge back comfortably in the family room, my own connector "harness" unprotestingly plugged in, despite the possible consequences to myself, my community, and my planet. Yet, as I sit here, I still wonder: "Is there anything more? More than this trio of evolved animal, cultural creature, and this clever and inventive species infatuated by consumerism and the by-products of science and technology?"

Quartet

Listening to the radio one evening, I found the music particularly relaxing and pleasing—even enchanting. The selections were from Handel's *Messiah*. I wish you too could have heard this particular broadcast. Some of the pieces had been recorded in 1941 by Marian Anderson, the famous American contralto. As she began her aria—"He shall feed his flock like a shepherd"—I suddenly felt both delight and praise for the composer and for this wonderful singer with such a gifted voice. I silently extended my compliments also to the music archivists, past inventors, and technical engineers who had caught her notes in mid-air two years before I was born and now transmitted them to me: "And He shall gather the lambs with His arms. . . ."

Her words rang in beauty. They resonated the bell of my soul. Can you explain how such music came to be, as if drawn magically from nature's cosmic hat?

And carry them in His bosom . . .
And gently lead those that are with young.

Lost in wonder, I sensed a lineage of care and love. Humans this time not mimicking wasps or wolves, nor inventing tools and technologies, but imitating the creative impulse itself, as if entering a new tonality layered with beauty, hovering close to some purpose and reward for being.

So what is our music, our ensemble within nature's ongoing variations? If you allow me to indulge in one final metaphor, I suggest that our format is not a trio but a full quartet of interlacing voices and songs taken both from our many past and present possibilities. To round out our cosmic journey, I pull out some of my favorite recordings—the string quartets by Beethoven.

How amazing these works are, how entrancing! Four players, four instruments, four tonal lines weaving in and out, twining harmonies, disharmonies, now floating heavenward, now earthward and back. Eventually the musical moment deepens until, after a variegated journey through time and tonality, the voices settle into a peaceful resolution.

In one of Beethoven's late quartets (number fifteen), the listener can enjoy his "Song of Thanksgiving," a musical psalm, composed in 1823 to celebrate his recovery from a long and debilitating illness. Here Beethoven walks the listener through a variety of tonalities. His mood is joyous and awake and, above all, supremely grateful to the forces that gave him, once again, a sense of life, health, and a

revitalization of his creative powers. "With a sense of renewed strength," he wrote on the original manuscript, and later, near the end, "with the most intimate feeling."[6]

In searching for a broad metaphor of life and meaning, I feel naturally drawn to this particular piece, Beethoven's "Song of Thanksgiving." If our metaphor's a quartet, what do the four voices represent?

Animal Ancestry

As we saw in the earlier sections of our galactic journey, one voice within our composition represents that ancient part of ourselves derived from our animal heritage, the traits, instincts, biochemical makeup, and genetically programmed responses, the so-called "shadows of forgotten ancestors," as the late Carl Sagan and his wife Ann Druyan called them in their book with the same title.[7] Humans still share many of these physical and psychological traits derived from our early relatives of the animal kingdom, traits retained over millions of years. *National Geographic* writer Susan Schiefelbein highlights the very oldest and deepest of these connections in her essay "The Cosmic Creature":

The salt in our bloodstreams and the calcium in our bones flowed in the first sea. . . . Preserved in the fossil record and in our bodies is evidence that all life is related to other life, that we take as our common ancestor the first single cell.[8]

I find it both personally insightful and psychologically satisfying to know I am directly connected to other animals through our ancestry, our common DNA and various hereditary traits, as well as our past mutual interactions with the natural world—our "co-evolutionary context." Commenting on this point, writer/philosopher David Abram reminds us that our minds and bodies

have formed themselves in delicate reciprocity with the man-ifold textures, sounds, and shapes of an animate earth . . . our eyes have evolved in subtle interaction with other eyes, as our ears are attuned by their very structure to the howl-ing of wolves and the honking of geese.[9]

Yet many of us seem to be strangers to this other world, oblivious to its subtle interplays and sensibilities as we go about our busy, noisy, fast-paced lifestyles. If we simply dismiss (or smother out) these connections, we may be inviting psychological damage—to be haunted perhaps by a peculiar loneliness and consequently to be incapable of feeling truly at home in the profoundest sense of that word.[10]

This loss may also make it difficult for us to begin to heal our combative relationship with those animals and plants we depend on and with whom we share the planet. Speaking more specifically on these points, Abram notes:

To shut ourselves off from these other voices, to continue by our lifestyles to condemn these other sensibilities to the oblivion of extinction, is to rob our own senses of their integrity, and to rob our minds of their coherence. We are human only in contact and conviviality with what is not human. Only in reciprocity with what is Other will be begin to heal ourselves.[11]

For the interested reader, good references on our animal ancestry include Sara Stein's *The Evolution Book* and Chet Raymo's *Biography of a Planet*. Loren Eiseley's beautifully crafted *The Immense Journey* (considered one of the classics on the subject) takes the armchair reader back, back, to our very earliest animal beginnings, as does Roger Lewin's book *Thread of Life*.

Each human embryo, for example, passes through a definite fish-like stage, eerily echoing our very ancient oceanic beginnings. Roger Lewin, in *Thread of Life*, comments on this intriguing developmental characteristic that, incidentally, applies not just to the human embryo, but also to the embryonic development of all mammals and reptiles:

> *every terrestrial vertebrate embryo for the past 300 million years has developed at some point a set of gill arches and blood vessels appropriate for it, just as its marine ancestors did in adult life. . . . Such reminders of the past history of a group of organisms are . . . about as good evidence of evolution as one could wish for. They reveal the ways in which the evolutionary process often puts old structures to new and unexpected uses.*[12]

The evolution of the human brain provides another example. Not only has our species developed a recent neocortex component (for reasoned thinking and symbolic abstraction), but we've also retained a more primitive component (the R-complex), responsible for activating essential survival behaviors from an earlier era, including such reptilian/mammalian traits as aggression, territoriality, and a tendency to conform to rigid social hierarchies.[13]

Like a separate musical part of a string quartet, this earlier "animal" part of ourselves[14] should not, I believe, be more or less important than any other component. If our metaphor for our makeup is music, with the composition being representative of the whole of our species, of our past and present possibilities, surely our early biological/genetic heritage is an integral part of that whole.

Cultural Capabilities

The second musical line is our cultural heritage, based on our malleable social and learning capabilities. Although other primate species have demonstrated an ability to use, even evolve, rudimentary culture,[15] humans have taken cultural interaction much further through our unique human family arrangements, gender roles, lineages, alliances, and our varied customs, rituals, traditional crafts, ceremonies, and many other forms of artistic expression.[16] A favorite book of mine on the variety of worldwide cultural adaptations is Marvin Harris's *Our Kind*.[17] I especially enjoyed Harris's ability to reconstruct a plausible scenario of a possible step-by-step continuum between (nonhuman) primate abilities and the protocultural/tool-making abilities of "our kind's" ancestors.

Another book, one that beautifully describes specific culture (Ladakh, in northern India), is Helena Norberg-Hodge's *Ancient Futures*.[18] Norberg-Hodge also contrasts the gap between an economically sustainable traditional culture and the Western technological nation-states whose overwhelming emphasis on growth and the materialistic ethic, she suggests, often leads to environmental degradation and social isolation.

Traditional culture, we discover, consists of *acquired* behaviors and beliefs, plus complex modes of communication. Who can guess, for example, the evolutionary impact of humankind's languages, in all their elasticity and complexity, from the stories, mythologies, songs, and poetry to the verbal dalliances of love and courting of our many ancestors? Again, this "voice" of our musical composition weaves through the piece on a basis of equality with the other voices. (There is no hierarchy among chamber musicians!)

Science and Technology

A third component is our relatively recent explosion of knowledge, including modern science and technology and our global systems of economic organization, each going far beyond anything resembling local or regional cultural adaptations of the past.

Take a moment to look about you. What do you see? Trace the origins of these artifacts from raw material extraction to design, engineering, and fabrication on through to their national (or international) dispersion and consumption. Again, one should emphasize that the long-range impact of these "advances" are often unpredictable and may have deleterious side effects unforeseen by the inventors. Despite obvious dangers to both nature and humanity, there's no doubt that the current level of our scientific knowledge and technologies (within life's long evolutionary time scale) is not only unique, but at times, a source of wonder, something truly new under the Sun. The late Carl Sagan, so beloved for his *Cosmos* series, spoke for many admirers of scientific discovery when, near the end of his life, he wrote:

> *Whenever I think about any of these discoveries, I feel a tingle of exhilaration. My heart races. I can't help it. Science is an astonishment and a delight. Every time a spacecraft flies by a new world, I find myself amazed.*[19]

As we know, science, with its amazing instruments, is now beginning to understand the smallest atomic particles. It has also examined minute genetic materials, and from far out in space, it's photographed the beautiful rings of Saturn (up close) and the birthing of baby stars and planets forming out of galactic dust. Astronomers have even recorded the original seeding matter of the universe of approximately fifteen billion years ago.

Of equal importance, science has studied ecological relationships, including principles of population growth and resource balance. Many feel that our species too must soon enter into true ecological harmony with Earth's web of life, just like the other creatures who reside with us on our small planet.

In this respect, humans (as the copycat species) must mimic not only individual plants (like the tenacious cocklebur) and animals (like the persistent squirrel), but must also imitate the techniques and evolve values for sustainable living within Earth's biological systems and finite resource boundaries. In other words, we must enter into what one writer calls "the Era of Ecology." Summarizing this point, poet Wendell Berry wrote:

> *We may, if we are able to make ourselves wise enough and humble enough, enter an "Era of Ecology," when we will utilize "the science of achieving an equilibrium with the environment." We will be as protective of the natural world as our primitive forebears, but this time for reasons that are knowledgeable and conscious rather than superstitious.*[20]

Exploring Values for a Sustainable Future

A helpful book for me, one that offers workable strategies, is David Orr's *Ecological Literacy*. Especially useful to those committed to exploring new values is the author's multidisciplinary approach, designed to help one understand our evolutionary past and to become versed on the interrelatedness of all life—here and now, locally and globally. These competencies then form a basis, a problem-solving infrastructure of discovering pathways eventually leading toward true sustainability:

> *Ecological literacy presumes that we understand our place in the story of evolution. It is to know that our health, well-being and ultimately our survival depend on working with, not against, natural forces. The basis of ecological literacy, then, is the comprehension of the interrelatedness of life grounded in the study of natural history, ecology, and thermodynamics.*[21]

As important as science is to an ecologically literate person, additional competencies may be gained by experiencing nature firsthand, of attaining an intimate familiarity, love, and appreciation for one's particular place on the planet. Ecological literacy may even at times be realized within spiritual or intuitive realms, by (re)discovering what

Orr describes as "the sense of wonder, the sheer delight in being alive in a beautiful, mysterious, bountiful world."[22]

Mystical Modality

The fourth musical line, the one that rounds out our quartet, is the capacity to experience the transcendent, to hear a mystical modality within the music. Some have called this state of awareness "cosmic consciousness."[23] Buddhists speak of "achieving Nirvana" (extinguishing worldly desire and delusion),[24] while the mystical Christian traditions refer to experiencing "the Kingdom of God within."[25]

American psychologist Abraham Maslow once interviewed individuals who had experienced unusual moments of clarity, of understanding themselves and their universe not in separateness but in a larger connectedness or unity in which the world appeared to be "not merely existent but also sacred."[26]

American naturalist and writer John Muir found his transcendent connection in nature; consider, for example, the following description from his essay "Twenty Hill Hollow":

> *If you are traveling for health, play truant to doctors and friends, fill your pocket with biscuits, and hide in the hills of the Hollow, lave in its waters, tan in its golds, bask in its flower-shine, and your baptisms will make you a new creature indeed . . . here will your hard doubts disappear, your carnal incrustations melt off, and your soul breathe deep and free in God's shoreless atmosphere of beauty and love. . . .*[27]

Nature was also the source of mystical inspiration for Henry Thoreau[28] and wildlife ecologist Aldo Leopold. What, for example, was the "music" that Leopold heard when he and a friend camped along a pristine wild river in Mexico? What was the "pulsing harmony" described so well in his essay "Song of the Gavilan"?

> *This song of the waters is audible to every ear, but there is other music in these hills, by no means audible to all. To hear*

even a few notes of it you must first live here for a long time,
and you must know the speech of hills and rivers. Then on a
still night, when the campfire is low and the Pleiades have
climbed over rimrocks, sit quietly and listen for a wolf to howl,
and think hard of everything you have seen and tried to under-
stand. Then you may hear it—a vast pulsing harmony—its
score inscribed on a thousand hills, its notes the lives and deaths
of plants and animals, its rhythms spanning the seconds
and the centuries.[29]

As a final example, astronomers and nonastronomers alike may have enjoyed memorable moments that conform to Aldous Huxley's feeling or conviction of the "ultimate allrightness of the universe":

The fact that in spite of pain, in spite of death, in spite of
all that happens which goes on all around us, this universe
is somehow all right.[30]

A pleasant thought! A wholesome thought to hold on to as Beethoven's "Song of Thanksgiving" nears its end, indeed, as we near the end of our explorations.

The quartet, for now, is over. Time for bed. For a few minutes, I linger about—feeling strangely happy—happy for this music and to have heard the song of the meadowlark earlier in the day. Happy too for my own consciousness and, stepping outside into the cool, fresh air, happy to see a half-moon beaming softly to the night from behind a distant pine.

May I too learn to sing and also to listen well, to treasure our music's intertwining and be thankful for each of its variegated voices? May I also enjoy a deeper connectedness to this existence, its pulse and mystery and to its everlasting ensemble—to keep humming along, mindful of a musical metaphor for both my time and place—indeed, a song of thanksgiving! Surely Beethoven must have sensed this. Even the Old Testament psalmist made it clear,

That I may publish with the voice of Thanksgiving
and tell of all thy wondrous works.[31]

and the Zen Master when he wrote,

When my life opens up very clearly,
I can't help, from the depths of my
heart, wanting to bow. . . .[32]

What's the meaning of it all? Indeed, what is the meaning of this music but pure, creative beauty and praise to all the forces that brought us life, health, and consciousness, and when we listen deeply, rounds out our cosmic journey and once again brings us home?

Endnotes

Preface

1. A term used by cosmologist and physicist Brian Swimme. See "Science as Wisdom: A Way Forward" (an interview with Swimme by Kurt de Boer) in *Earth Light,* Summer, 1997, page 10.

Chapter 4: High Jumping

1. George A. Sheehan, *Dr. Sheehan on Running* (Mountain View, CA: World Publisher, 1975), p. 190.

2. Eugen Herrigel, *Zen in the Art of Archery* (New York: Vintage, 1971), p. 41.

Chapter 6: The Coming Repair Age

1. Christopher Williams, *Craftsman of Necessity* (New York: Vintage, 1974), p. 91.

2. B. Coburn, "Nepali Aama," *The Coevolutionary Quarterly,* Spring, 1980, pp. 104-105.

Chapter 8: Craftsmanship and Salvation

1. Quoted from Elizabeth Drew's Poetry, *A Modern Guide to Its Understanding and Enjoyment* (New York: Dell, 1959), pp. 19-20.

2. Robert M. Pirsig, *Zen and the Art of Motorcycle Maintenance* (New York: Bantam, 1974), p. 91.

3. Henry David Thoreau, *Walden* (New York: Bramall House, 1951), p. 348.

Chapter 9: Simplify, Simplify: Henry Thoreau as Economic Prophet

1. *Ibid.*, p. 19.

2. Henry David Thoreau, *The Journal of Henry David Thoreau*, ed. by R. Torrey, F. Allen (New York: Dover, 1962), journal entry from July 5th, 1852.

3. *Walden*, p. 67.

4. *Ibid.*, p. 66.

5. *Ibid.*, p. 68.

6. *Ibid.*, p. 148.

7. *Ibid.*, p. 337.

8. Walter Harding, *The Days of Henry David Thoreau* (New York: Dover, 1982), p. 286.

9. *Walden*, p. 106.

10. *Ibid.*, p. 106.

11. *Ibid.*, p. 29.

12. *Journal*, July 19th, 1851.

13. *Walden*, p. 86.

14. *Ibid.*, p. 45.

Chapter 11: A Cosmic Journey

1. For those who are unfamiliar with the night sky, an inexpensive cardboard star chart would be helpful to identify the various constellations mentioned in this chapter.

2. Daniel Whitmire and Ray Reynolds, "The Fiery Fate of the Solar System," *Astronomy*, April 1990, p. 29.

3. The Orion Nebula (best seen in winter) is located in the middle part of the great Hunter's sword. Look under his bright three-star belt (and to the upper left of the bright star Rigel representing one of the Hunter's legs). With medium-power magnification, one can just make out four tiny stars arranged in a trapezoid shape; these are new stellar creations, perhaps only 25,000 years old, still in the process of forming. As a group, astronomers call this quartet of stars the "Trapezium." See *Natural History*, Jan. 1996, p. 57.

4. C.S. Lewis, *The Four Loves* (New York: Harcourt Brace Jovanovich, 1960), pp. 56-57.

5. Lao-tzu, *The Way of Life*, trans. by R.B. Blakney (New York: American Library, 1955), p. 56.

6. K.L. Reichelt, *Meditation and Piety in the Far East* (New York: Harper & Bros., 1954), p. 41.

7. This story, narrated by Kiowa/Caddo tribesperson Mary Bombadier, was taken from *Legends in Stone, Bone, and Wood*, by Tsonakwa and Yolaikia (Minneapolis: Arts and Learning Services Foundation, 1986), p. 14.

8. *Ibid.*, p. 14. Compare Maheo's creative clap with the Hindu creation story where Brahman (or Spirit) also feels the urge to create something out of nothing: "In the beginning—when there was no creation—there was Spirit. But Spirit wanted to create, and by His wishful thought He projected a great sphere of light, or cosmic energy which became the universe" (P. Yogananda, *Man's Eternal Quest*, p. 299, Los Angeles: Self-Realization Fellowship, 1988).

9. The reason why the Big Bang theory is currently the best scientific explanation for the origin of the universe can be seen in Neil de Grasse Tyson's "In Defense of the Big Bang," *Natural History*, Dec. 96-Jan. 97, p. 76.

10. Chet Raymo, *The Soul of the Night* (New York: Prentice Hall, 1985), p. 46.

11. Readers that are curious about the recent scientific speculations on what might have occurred prior to the Big Bang should refer to the Michio Kaku piece, "What Happened Before the Big Bang?" (*Astronomy*, May 1996, pp. 36-41).

12. Gary Bennett, "Cosmic Origins of the Elements," *Astronomy*, Aug. 1988, p. 18.

13. Raymo, p. 47.

14. Personal correspondence, Sept. 20, 1990.

15. Bennett, p. 20.

16. Terrence Dickinson, *Exploring the Night Sky* (Ontario: Camden House, 1987), p. 44, and "A Beast in the Core," by Marcia Bartusiak in *Astronony*, July, 1998, pp. 42-47.

17. See George Smoot and Keay Davidson, *Wrinkles in Time* (New York: Avon Books, 1993).

18. Patrick Moore, *Armchair Astronomy* (New York: Norton, 1984), p. 128.

19. Raymo, p. 102.

20. An excellent book to help locate the sights mentioned is *Discover the Stars* by Richard Berry (New York: Harmony Books, 1987). For information on Sagittarius, see pp. 84-85.

21. Although binoculars are helpful, the Andromeda spiral is faintly visible with the naked eye on a dark moonless night. In fact, from Northern latitudes, Andromeda is the only object that can be seen (without optical assistance) that's not a part of our own Milky Way.

22. Fine photographs of the Great Andromeda spiral galaxy can be seen in a number of books. The inexpensive *Golden Guide to Stars* (New York: Golden Press, 1985) by H. S. Zim is one good source (p. 43). A series of exceptionally beautiful photos of Andromeda can be found in Timothy Ferris' *Galaxies* (New York: Stewart, Tabori, & Chang, 1982), pp. 77-79.

23. Louise B. Young, *The Blue Planet* (Boston: Little Brown, 1983), p. 266.

Chapter 12: Of Time and Place

1. Although a group of local history buffs tried to save Colfax's original water tower, maintenance cost and liability considerations decided its ultimate fate. Once every reasonable effort had been made to preserve the structure, loss perhaps should not be seen as a depressing failure, but "accepted" as a part of universal change: "View the process as a lesson in impermanence" a Nepalese Buddhist monk advised a group confronted with a similar situation. (See "Stupas Along the Rio Grande" by Anna Racicot, *Tricycle*, Summer, 1997, p. 63.)

2. The 3.5-billion-year-old fossils were found near the small town of Marble Bar in western Australia by UCLA paleobiologist J. William Schopf. Microscopic photographs of strands of these organisms can be seen in Wallace Ravven's, "In the Beginning;" (*Discover*, Oct., 1990, pp. 98-101). Evidence points to perhaps even older fossils (3.8 billion years old) found on Akilia Island near Greenland. See *Science News*, Nov. 9, 1996, p. 292.

3. For more details, see Gould, *Wonderful Life*.

4. Psalm 90:12.

5. Psalm 104: 15-16.

6. Roger Lewin, *In the Age of Mankind* (Washington. D.C.: Smithsonian Institution, 1988), p. 122.

7. Alexander Marshack, "Exploring the Mind of Ice Age Man," *National Geographic*, Jan. 1975, pp. 66-67.

8. John J. Putman, "The Search for Modern Humans," *National Geographic*, Oct. 1988, p. 449. The oldest bone flute, made from a juvenile bear's thighbone and associated with Neanderthals, may date back as far as 43,000 to 82,000 years ago. (See "Neanderthal Noisemaker," *Science News*, Nov. 23, 1996, p. 328.)

9. One excavation in Germany indicated that wooden spears (made from the trunk of a spruce) may date back as far as 400,000 years ago. See "German Mine Yields Ancient Hunting Spears," *Science News*, Mar. 1, 1997, p. 134.

10. See Richard Monastersky, "Out of Arid Africa," *Science News*, Aug. 3, 1996, p. 74.

11. Tim Folger, "The Naked and the Bipedal," *Discover*, Nov. 1993, p. 34.

12. *Ibid.*, p. 35.

13. Lewin, pp. 50-56. Also see, Donald Johanson and Maitland Edey, *Lucy, the Beginnings of Humankind* (New York: Warner, 1981).

14. See Richard Leakey's *The Making of Mankind* (New York: E. P. Dutton, 1981), pp. 88-95. Among evolutionary biologists, there are, of course, ongoing disagreements. For example, an alternative hypothesis to the savanna food-sharing theory comes from chimpanzee studies in the rain forests of the Ivory Coast where researchers observed chimps sharing food and also using a variety of primitive tools. See "Dim Forest, Bright Chimps," by Christopher Boesch and Hedwidge Boeash-Achermann, *Natural History*, Sept., 1991, pp. 50-57.

15. Edward O. Wilson, *Biophilia* (Cambridge: Harvard University Press, 1984), p. 110.

16. Note that the very earliest primates date back to about seventy million years ago; roughly the size (and active disposition) of a squirrel, these little mammals were basically tree-dwellers that spent their night hours scampering about for small insects.

17. Carl Sagan, *The Dragons of Eden* (New York: Ballantine Books, 1977), p. 87.

18. May Theilgaard Watts, *Reading the Landscape of America* (New York: Macmillan, 1975), pp. 1-4.

19. See "How did *Archaeopteryx* cross the road?" by Scott Fields, *Earth*, Feb. 1995, p. 18.

20. John C. McLoughlin, *Synapsida—A New Look into the Origins of Mammals* (New York: Viking, 1980).

21. See "The Lost Tribe of the Mammals" by Richard Monastersky (*Science News*, Dec. 14, 1996, p. 378).

22. To explore the possibilities of night peripheral vision, see Nelson Zink and Stephen Parks, "Nightwalking: Exploring the Dark with Peripheral Vision," in *Whole Earth Review*, Fall, 1991, pp. 4-9.

23. McLoughlin, p. 100.

24. See "Tripping Over History" by Jeffrey Kluger (*Discover*, Dec. 1990, pp. 40-41.)

25. An excellent summary of this "earth altering" event can be seen in the article "The Day the Dinosaurs Died" by Ron Cowen (*Astronomy*, Aug. 3, 1996, pp. 34-41).

26. Raymo, p. 104.

27. Paleobotanist Henk Visscher of the Utrecht University in the Netherlands believes the Permian mass extinction was caused by massive volcanic eruptions in Siberia that spread basalt over large areas of the earth. Carbon dioxide and acidic gases would also have contributed to the mass killings. See *Science News*, Mar. 16, 1996 (p. 164) and May 16, 1998 (p. 308).

28. *Simon & Schuster's Guide to Fossils* (New York: Simon & Schuster, 1986), entry 154.

29. John Reader, *The Rise of Life* (New York: Knopf, 1986), p. 65.

30. Some researchers suggest that there may have been microscopic land life in the form of microbial mats (cyanobacteria) as long ago as a billion years ago. Not all paleobiologists agree however. See Daniel Pendick's "The Precambrian Golf Course," *Earth*, Sept. 1994, pp. 20-23.

31. "Fossils Push Back Origin of Land Animals," by R. Monastersky (*Science News*, Nov. 10, 1990, p. 138).

32. Raymo, p. 91.

33. Other candidates for the earliest chordate include *Yunnanozoon*, from fossils found near Chengjiang China that date to some 530 million years ago. (See "Vertebrate Origins: The fossils speak up" in *Science News*, Feb. 3, 1996, p. 75), and *Cathaymyrus diadexus* also found in China of 535 million years ago; (see "New Fossil Worms In," *Earth*, Apr. 1997, p. 12).

34. Gould, pp. 321-323. Also see "Explosion of Life: The Cambrian Period," by Rick Gore, *National Geographic*, October 1993, pp. 120-136.

35. Loren Eiseley, *The Immense Journey* (New York: Vintage, 1957), p. 203.

36. Speculation on the requisite chemical sequences necessary to begin self-replicating primitive life-forms can be found in Anthony Mellerish's article, "The Origin of Life," in *Natural History*, June, 1994, pp. 10-15.

37. Charles Darwin, *Origin of Species* (New York: New American Library, 1958), p. 450.

Chapter 13: The Copycat Species

1. Stephen Jay Gould, "The Golden Rule—A Proper Scale for Our Environmental Crisis," *Natural History*, Sept. 1990, p. 28.

2. Bill Holm, *Boxelder Bug Variations—A Meditation on an idea in Language and Music* (Minneapolis: Milkweed Editions, 1985), p. 57.

3. According to the fossil record, evidence of the oldest complex organisms appear to be wormlike creatures that made burrows in the 800-million-year-old Buckingham Sandstone of northern Australia. See Roger Lewin's *Thread of Life* (New York: W. W. Norton, 1982), p. 115.

4. Howard R. Feldman, "Against all Odds," *Earth*, July 1992, p. 30.

5. Richard Byrne, author of *The Thinking Ape*, defines thinking (as an aspect of intelligence) as "a process that can take known information and work it out, that is, simulate or imagine the consequences of change that haven't happened in the real world." (See "These Animals Think, Therefore . . ." by Meredith F. Small; *Natural History*, Aug. 8, 1996, p. 29.)

6. Jane van Lawick-Goodall, *My Friends, the Wild Chimpanzees* (Washington, D.C.: National Geographic Society, 1967), pp. 32-34.

7. Bernd Heinrich, "Nutcracker Sweets," *Natural History*, Feb. 1991, p. 8.

8. For an interesting parallel of a squirrel (or bird, etc.) as a "teacher," see *The Sacred Pipe: Black Elk's Account of the Seven Rites of the Ogalala Sioux*, ed. by Joseph Epes Brown (Baltimore: Penguin, 1971). Referring to these animal/teachers (or "people"), Black Elk comments: "All these people are important, for in their own way they are wise and they can teach us two-leggeds much if we make ourselves humble before them" (p. 58).

9. Taken from the Old Testament: Job 12:7-8.

10. This quote is from Ortega y Gasset's *Prologo a un Tratado de Monteria*, reprinted in C. W. Ceram's, *The First American* (New York: New American Library, 1971), pp. 320-321.

11. Heinrich, p. 8.

12. See "Wasp" entry in *The World Book Encyclopedia* (Chicago: Field Enterprises, 1966), p. 87.

13. Joanne Demski, "An Old Twist on Exercise," *The Milwaukee Sentinel*, July 21, 1990, Part 3, p. 1.

14. Pandit Usharbudh Arya, *Philosophy of Hatha Yoga* (Honesdale Penn: The Himalayan International Institute, 1977), p. 75.

15. See *Tai Chi Handbook* by Herman Kanz (Garden City: Dolphin, 1974), pp. 10-11.

16. Millicent E. Selsam, *Plants that Heal* (New York: William Morrow, 1959), p. 14.

17. John Lame Deer and Richard Erdoes, *Lame Deer: Seeker of Visions* (New York: Washington Square Press, 1972), pp. 153-154.

18. John Muir, *The Story of My Boyhood and Youth* (Madison, WI.: The University of Wisconsin Press, 1965), pp. 101-102.

19. *U.S. News and World Report*, Aug. 10, 1987, p. 6. Another example of an amphibian's contribution to medicine is the dumpy frog of southern New Guinea, a creature that provides science with a compound that has proven to be effective against herpes simplex (see "Vanishing Frogs" by Jon R. Luoma in *Audubon*, May/June, 1997, p. 69).

20. See "Amphibian Alarm: Just Where Have all the Frogs Gone?" by Beth Livermore (*Smithsonian*, Oct. 1992, pp. 113-120).

21. Ozone depletion and the consequent increase in UV-B radiation is apparently one of the reasons for some of the frog and toad species' decline. See Andrew R. Blaustein's article "Amphibians in a Bad Light" (*Natural History*, Oct. 1994; pp. 32-39).

22. Taken from Public Broadcasting System's "The Cuban Missile Crisis, at the Brink." Broadcast in October, 1992.

23. Thich Nhat Hanh, *Touching Peace* (Berkeley: Parallax Press, 1992), pp. 16, 18, 48.

24. "Relax . . . Relax . . . You Are Feeling Very Original," *Business Week*, Sept., 30, 1985, p. 84.

25. Velcro was *first* invented by Georges de Mestral, a Swiss engineer, in 1948. According to plant ecologist Robert Read, the natural analogy was also a factor; de Mestral saw the "fastening" possibilities "as he combed cockleburs from his dog after an autumn walk through the alpen countryside. . . ." See Read's "Of Burs and Beagles," *Wisconsin Natural Resources*, Aug. 1991, p. 6.

Chapter 14: Music, Metaphor and Meaning

1. "The American Road," produced by the Ford Motor Company, 1974.

2. Quoted from Emerson's 1847 poem, "Ode: Inscribed to W. H. Channing;" Ralph Waldo Emerson, *Selected Prose and Poetry*, ed. Reginald L. Cook (New York: Holt, Rinehart & Winston, 1962), p. 381.

3. Thoreau, *Walden*, p. 51.

4. E.F. Schumacher, *Small Is Beautiful* (New York: Perennial Library, 1973), p. 7.

5. All quotes taken from Jerry Mander's *In the Absence of the Sacred* (San Francisco: Sierra Club Books, 1991), pp. 43-44.

6. Joseph de Marliave, *Beethoven's Quartets* (New York: Dover, 1961), pp. 328-355. The English translations from the German were taken from the record jacket notes of the Budapest's Quartet's recording of Beethoven Quartet No. 15, Opus 132 (New York: Columbia Masterwork, ML 4586).

7. Carl Sagan and Ann Druyan, *Shadows of Forgotten Ancestors: A Search for Who We Are* (New York: Random House, 1992).

8. Quoted from *The Incredible Machine* (Washington, D.C.: The National Geographic Society, 1986), p. 11.

9. David Abram, *The Spell of the Sensuous: Perception and Language in a More-Than-Human World* (New York: Pantheon Books, 1996), p.22. In reading Abram's book, I have found no better description of the potential for, and value of, re-experiencing our age-old animal connections, and also why this component of our "quartet" is so important to our mental (and environmental) health.

10. Perhaps no one has written more beautifully on the meaning of being "at home" in nature than Henry Thoreau; see particularly his chapter on "Solitude" in *Walden*. Often quoted is the opening paragraph which begins, "This is a delicious evening when the whole body is one sense, and imbibes delight through every pore. I go and come with a strange liberty in Nature, a part of herself. . . ." (p. 261).

11. Abram, p. 22.

12. Lewin, *Thread of Life*, p 62.

13. Sagan, *Dragons of Eden*, p. 63. See also Helen Fisher, *The Sex Contract* (New York: Quill, 1983), pp. 186-187.

14. Some of the negative aspects of our genetic "animal component," which some writers have seen as the probable source of warfare and other brutalities of human against human, are well documented in Lyall Watson's disturbing book *Dark Nature: A Natural History of Evil* (New York: Harper Perennial, 1997). Watson, I believe, does a service to help us better understand biological tendencies that can, perhaps, be inhibited by culture, progressive institutions, and rule of law.

15. See Sagan and Druyan, *Shadows of Forgotten Ancestors*, pp. 373-377.

16. Perhaps the cultural component needs are recognized when people take time to explore their "roots" through family genealogy and begin to appreciate the traditional culture of their ancestors. Also, martial arts, with their emphasis on ritual and ceremonials are another route for nontraditional Westerners to experience the meaning and pleasure associated with the cultural "voice" within us. See, for example, George Leonard's *Mastery* (New York: Plume, 1992).

17. Marvin Harris, *Our Kind* (New York: Harper, 1989).

18. Helena Norberg-Hodge, *Ancient Futures* (San Francisco: Sierra Club Books, 1991).

19. Carl Sagan, *The Demon-Haunted World* (New York: Ballantine, 1997), p. 330.

20. Wendell Berry, *A Continuous Harmony* (New York: Harcourt Brace Jovanovich, 1972), p. 12. The term "Era of Ecology" and reference quotes are from John S. Collis, *The Triumph of the Tree* (New York: The Viking Press, 1954), pp. ix-x. See also Paul Hawken's *The Ecology of Commerce* (New York: HarperCollins, 1993) for a discussion on sustainable business practices.

21. David W. Orr, *Ecological Literacy* (Albany: State University of New York Press, 1992) p. 93.

22. *Ibid.*, p. 86.

23. Richard Maurice Bucke, *Cosmic Consciousness* (Secaucus, NJ: Citadel Press, 1973), pp. 178-196.

24. See Nancy Wilson Ross's *Buddhism: A Way of Life and Thought* (New York: Vintage, 1980), p. 47. Other fine commentaries on Buddhist methods of meditation and mindfulness can be found in Thich Nhat Hanh's *Peace Is Every Step* (New York: Bantam, 1991) and H. Saddhatissa's *The Buddha's Way* (New York: George Braziller, 1972).

25. Peace Pilgrim, *Peace Pilgrim, Her Life and Work in Her Own Words* (Santa Fe: Ocean Tree, 1983), p. 86. More specifically see Luke 17:21.

26. Abraham H. Maslow, *Religions, Values, and Peak-Experiences* (New York: Penguin, 1976), pp. 59, 65.

27. John Muir, *Wilderness Essays* (Salt Lake City: Peregrine Smith, 1980), p. 87.

28. See, for example, William J. Wolf's *Thoreau: Mystic, Prophet, Ecologist* (Philadelphia: Pilgrim Press, 1974).

29. Aldo Leopold, *A Sand County Almanac* (London: Oxford University Press, 1949), p. 149.

30. Quoted from the essay "Visionary Experience" by Aldous Huxley, taken from *The Highest State of Consciousness*, ed. by John White (New York: Doubleday, 1972), p. 49.

31. Psalms, 26:7

32. Hara Akegarasu, "O New Year!" *Zen Notes*, Jan. 1975, p. 2.

Index